Artificial Intelligence

extbook

As per CBSE Syllabus Code 417

6

Harmeet Kaur
M. Anhitha

FIRST EDITION 2021

ISBN: 978-93-90684-304

REPRINT 2025

LIMITS OF LIABILITY AND DISCLAIMER OF WARRANTY

Distributors:

BPB PUBLICATIONS
20, Ansari Road, Darya Ganj
New Delhi-110002
Ph: 23254990/23254991

DECCAN AGENCIES
4-3-329, Bank Street,
Hyderabad-500195
Ph: 24756967/24756400

MICRO MEDIA
Shop No. 5, Mahendra Chambers,
150 DN Rd. Next to Capital Cinema,
V.T. (C.S.T.) Station, MUMBAI-400 001
Ph: 22078296/22078297

BPB BOOK CENTRE
376 Old Lajpat Rai Market,
Delhi-110006
Ph: 23861747

To View Complete BPB Publications Catalogue Scan the QR Code:

Published by Manish Jain for BPB Publications, 20 Ansari Road, Darya Ganj, New Delhi-110002 and Printed at Manipal Technologies Ltd., Karnataka (India)

www.bpbonline.com

Dedicated to

Our parents, family members, peers & dear students.

About the Authors

Harmeet Kaur is currently working as Senior Computer Teacher, Department of Computer Science at Heritage Xperiential Learning School, Gurugram. She has over 23 years of experience in the field of education; teaching Computer Science, Informatics Practices and Multimedia and Web Technologies to grades XI and XII along with a background of mentoring, IT curriculum development for STEM integration, and staff training and development. She has led various in-house projects such as Learning Management System to propagate collaborative personalized e-Learning. She is well adept in Google Apps for Education and uses it as a primary platform for her classroom teaching. She integrates multiple teaching styles to build digital literacy skills in millennial learners while strongly promoting safe and ethical use of technology. She believes in driving the experiential and project-based pedagogy by imparting mobile computing skills to high school students. She has conducted various workshops in and around Delhi-NCR to train teachers with latest pedagogies of classroom management, incorporating Tech to teach STEM education and "learning by doing" hands-on workshops. She has authored training material for in-house teacher training and been constructive in ICT curriculum development.

LinkedIn: linkedin.com/in/harmeetkaur2504

Website: www.harmeetkaur.in

M. Anhitha has an overall professional experience of more than 9 years. She has written many books including Fundamentals of computer science, Information Technology and currently working as a writer in computer science where she collaborates and works with enthusiasts across the globe. She has done B.Tech in Information Technology and M.Tech in Computer Science. She likes to keep herself updated to the latest trends and technologies.

LinkedIn: linkedin.com/in/m-anhitha-234130206

Blog: https://taartech.blogspot.com/

Acknowledgements

We would like to express our gratitude to everyone at BPB Publications for giving us this opportunity to write the book. We are thankful to all the resource persons at BPB Publications for editing, technical reviewing and language editing the book.

We are thankful to each other and our families for being supportive in numerous ways and for giving their unconditional love and support at all times.

Lastly, but not the least, we would like to thank God for bearing us with courage and humility to be able to write this book for our students.

— *Harmeet Kaur*

— *M. Anhitha*

Preface

Artificial intelligence (AI) studies human behaviour and creates machines that can demonstrate human like behaviours (learn, plan and solve problems) with minimal human interference. AI has been a vast subject which focuses on some of the major topics such as automation, computer vision, facial recognition systems, game artificial intelligence, hybrid intelligent system, problem solving, machine learning, and natural language understanding and so on.

This book is divided into three chapters and provides a detailed description of the basic concepts of Artificial Intelligence.

Chapter 1 explains what is Artificial Intelligence, its applications in their daily lives. Further it shows how Data for Artificial Intelligence, Natural Language Processing, and Computer Vision is related.

Chapter 2 provides a detailed explanation of smart homes, its applications. Further it explains about inklewriter and how to write an interactive story using it.

Chapter 3 focuses on Sustainable Development Goals. Further the emerging trends in different fields which are getting affected by AI is explained.

Throughout the book many activities have been given in the chapter to understand the concept in a better way.

Project on:

- Smarter home, Smarter hospitals.
- Draw a floorplan using LucidChart.
- Create an Automatic Door Unlocking system using Face Recognition in Pictoblox has been given to understand the concept in a better way.

One **Sample paper** with solutions has been given to practice.

Key terms in the form of **glossary** have been given to enhance the learning.

Syllabus for Middle School (class VI/VII/VIII)

INTRODUCTION TO ARTIFICIAL INTELLIGENCE

OBJECTIVES OF THE MODULE:

This module of Artificial Intelligence focuses on:

- Helping learners understand the world of Artificial Intelligence and its applications through games, activities, and multi-sensorial learning to become AI-Ready.
- Allowing the learners to construct the meaning of AI through interactive participation and engaging hands-on activities.

OUTLINE CURRICULUM:

MODULE	SUB-UNIT	DURATION
Introduction to Artificial Intelligence	Excite	2.5 Hours
	Relate	02 Hours
	Purpose	02 Hours
	Possibilities	02 Hours
	AI Ethics	3.5 Hours
TOTAL DURATION		**12 hours**
TOTAL MARKS		**50 marks (Theory = 15 + Practical 35)**

DETAILED CURRICULUM:

SUB-UNIT	LEARNING OUTCOMES	SESSION / ACTIVITY / PRACTICAL
1. EXCITE	• To identify and appreciate Artificial Intelligence and describe its applications in daily life.	Session: Introduction to AI and setting up the context of the curriculum Ice Breaker Activity: Dream Smart Home idea Learners to design a rough layout of floor plan of their dream smart home.
	• To relate, apply and reflect on the Human-Machine Interactions. • To identify and interact with the three domains of AI: Data, Computer Vision and Natural Language Processing.	Recommended Activity: The AI Game Learners' to participate in three games based on different AI domains. • Game 1: Rock, Paper and Scissors (based on data) • Game 2: Mystery Animal (based on Natural Language Processing - NLP) • Game 3: Emoji Scavenger Hunt (based on Computer Vision - CV)

	• To undergo an assessment for analysing progress towards acquired AI-Readiness skills.	Recommended Activity: AI Quiz (Paper Pen/Online Quiz)
	• To imagine, examine and reflect on the skills required for futuristic job opportunities.	Recommended Activity: Writing a Letter to one's future self Learners to write a letter to self-keeping the future in context. They will describe what they have learnt so far or what they would like to learn someday
2. RELATE	• Learners' to relate to application of Artificial Intelligence in their daily lives	Video Session: To watch a video Introducing the concept of Smart Cities, Smart Schools and Smart Homes
	• To unleash their imagination towards smart homes and build an interactive story around it. • To relate, apply and reflect on the Human–Machine interactions.	Recommended Activity: Write an Interactive Story Learners' to draw a floor plan of a Home/ School/ City and write an interactive story around it using the Story Speaker extension in Google docs.
3. PURPOSE	• To understand the impact of Artificial Intelligence on Sustainable Development Goals to develop responsible citizenship.	Session: Introduction to UN Sustainable Development Goals Recommended Activity: Go Goals Board Game Learners to answer questions on Sustainable Development Goals
4. POSSIBILITIES	• To research and develop awareness of skills required for jobs of the future. • To imagine, examine and reflect on the skills required for the futuristic opportunities. • To develop effective communication and collaborative work skills.	Session: Theme-based research and Case Studies Learners will listen to various case-studies of inspiring start-ups, companies or communities where AI has been involved in real-life. Learners will be allotted a theme around which they need to search for present AI trends and have to visualise the future of AI in and around their respective theme. Recommended Activity: Job Ad Creating activity Learners to create a job advertisement for a firm describing the nature of job available and the skill-set required for it 10 years down the line. They need to figure out how AI is going to transform the nature of jobs and create the Ad accordingly.

5. AI ETHICS	• To understand and reflect on the ethical issues around AI.	Video Session: Discussing about AI Ethics Recommended Activity: Ethics Awareness Students play the role of major stakeholders and they have to decide what is ethical and what is not for a given scenario.
	• To gain awareness around AI bias and AI access.	Session: AI Bias and AI Access • Discussing about the possible bias in data collection • Discussing about the implications of AI technology
	• To let the students analyse the advantages and disadvantages of Artificial Intelligence.	Recommended Activity: Balloon Debate Students divide in teams of 3 and 2 teams are given the same theme. One team goes in affirmation to AI for their section while the other one goes against it. They have to come up with their points as to why AI is beneficial/ harmful for the society.

Contents

1 INTRODUCTION TO ARTIFICIAL INTELLIGENCE

Structure Bot

In this chapter, we will discuss:

- The meaning of the term Artificial Intelligence
- Applications of Artificial Intelligence
- Advantages and Disadvantages of Artificial Intelligence

Objective Bot

At the end of this chapter, you should be able to:

- Know the use of AI in various applications
- Learn about Natural Language Processing and Computer Vision
- Understand the applications of Natural Language Processing and Computer Vision

Introduction to Artificial Intelligence

Artificial intelligence (AI) is an intelligence which is demonstrated by machines.

A quip in Tesler's Theorem says "*AI is whatever hasn't been done yet.*"

Modern machine capabilities explain that AI include in:

- Understanding human speech
- Competing at the highest level in strategic game systems (chess)
- Automatically operating cars
- Intelligent routing in content delivery networks
- Military simulations

Fact Bot

Artificial Intelligence is when a computer program or machine can think and learn.

Activity I

See-Saw

Description

- In this game there are seesaws and some objects of different shapes are placed on it.
- When two objects are placed on the two sides of a seesaw, the side which touches the ground has the heavier object.
- You need to select the heavy object form the list of objects shown and balance the seesaw.
- There will be more than one seesaw so you need to make multiple comparisons to find out the heaviest item.

Instruction

- Game has total 20 levels.
- Each level comes with seesaw, containing objects of different weight.
- You need to select the object of heavy weight to balance the seesaw.

To play the game:

1. Go to the link: https://www.proprofsgames.com/seesaw-logic/
2. The following screen appear:

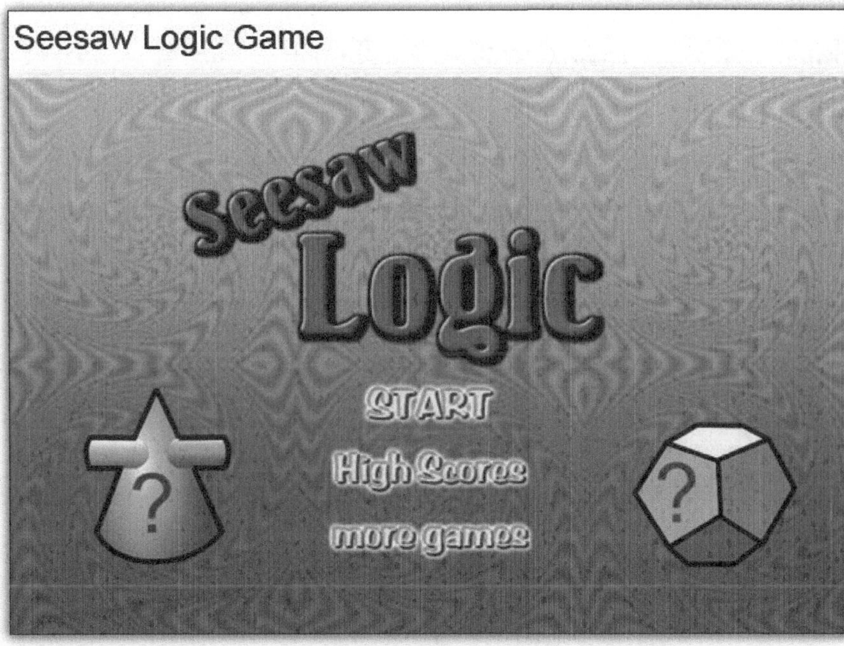

3. Click on START.
4. Instruction page will appear showing:

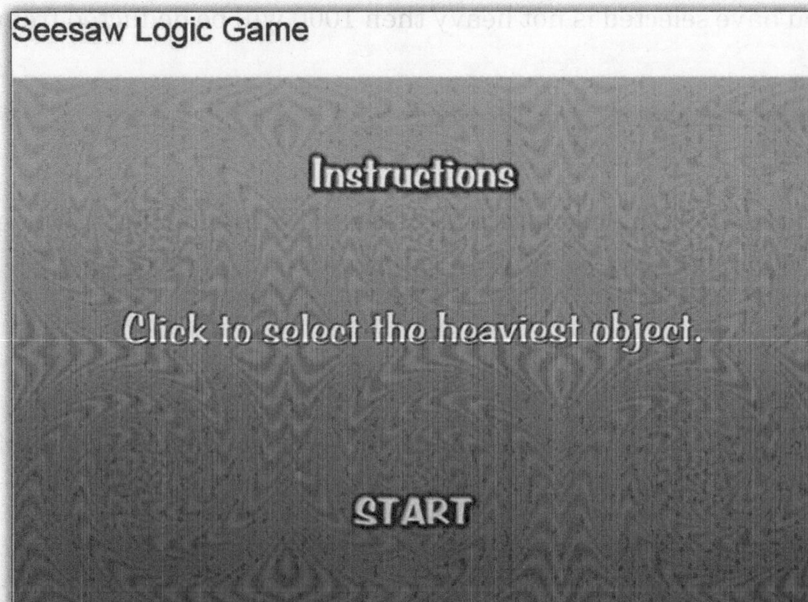

5. Click on START.
6. The following screen appears:

You need to select the heaviest object form the bottom to balance the seesaw.

7. If you select the correct object then your score will be 1000, and in case if the object you have selected is not heavy then 1000 will be deducted from your score.

Why AI field was founded?

AI field was founded on the assumption that human intelligence "*can be so precisely described that a machine can be made to simulate it*".

What is Artificial Intelligence?

Artificial Intelligence (AI) was first coined in 1956 at Dartmouth Conference by a cognitive scientist, **John McCarthy**, at the Dartmouth Conference.

Artificial intelligence (AI) refers to the simulation of human intelligence in the machines which are programmed to think like humans and mimic the actions of humans.

DEFINITION

Artificial intelligence is a way in which a machine can copy the actions performed by humans and execute the task of humans.

Activity II

Rubic Cube Game

Description

- Game is to rotate the sides of the cube to make the sides with one color of 9*9 matrix.
- You need to click on the scramble button with the cursor on right side of screen to begin the game.
- Click/drag on corner block of the side of cube to turn the side.
- To rotate the whole cube, drag the center block of any row with the cursor.
- Continue to turn sides until the puzzle is solved.

Instruction

- You need to rotate the rows so that the each row of the faces of the cube has only one single colour.
- To rotate the row, click the arrows and drag the cube to turn it around.

To play the game:

1. Visit the link: https://www.proprofsgames.com/rubic-cube/
2. The following screen appear:

Rubic Cube Game

3. Click on START.
4. Now the move the arrow, to make the one sides of cube of same color, your time and move will be displayed on the left side of the screen.

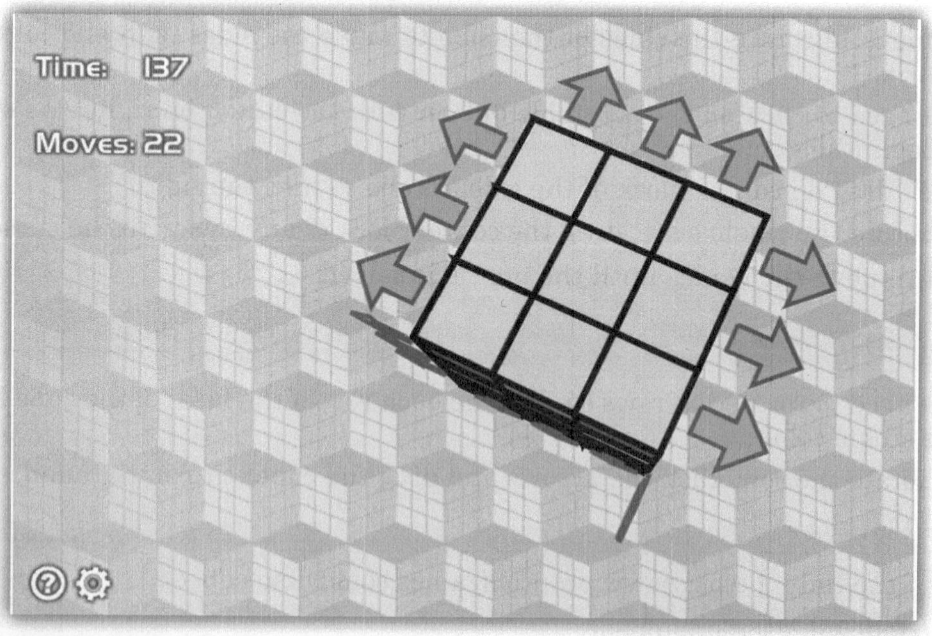

Applications of AI

Marketing

With AI we have an algorithm or a bot for the purpose of marketing a brand or a company.

Example: Finding the movies on Netflix.

Banking

Banks use AI-based systems to provide customer support, detect anomalies and credit card frauds.

Finance

Financial organizations are turning to AI to improve their stock trading performance and boost profit.

Agriculture

AI can help farmers to get more from the land while using resources more sustainably. Issues such as climate change, population growth, and food security concerns have pushed the industry into seeking more innovative approaches to improve crop yield.

Health Care

When it comes to saving our lives, a lot of organizations and medical care centres are relying on AI.

Coala life, a company that has a digitalized device that can find cardiac diseases.

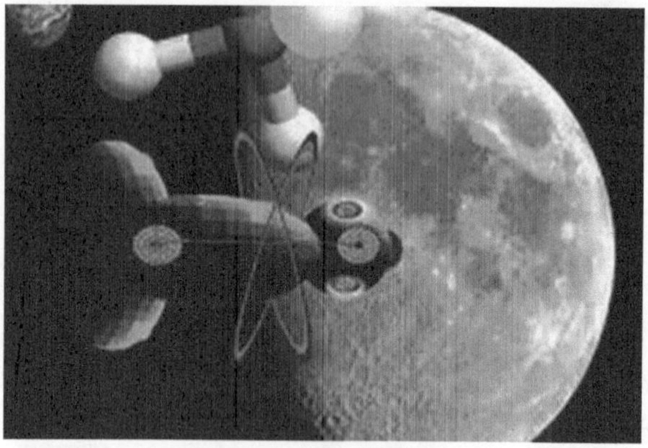

Space Exploration

Astronomers used Artificial Intelligence to sift through years of data obtained by the Kepler telescope in order to identify a distant eight-planet solar system.

Autonomous Vehicles/ Self driving cars/ Driverless cars

Self-driving cars have been a buzzword in the AI industry. The AI system collects data from the vehicles radar, cameras, GPS, and cloud services to produce control signals that operate the vehicle.

Another famous example of an autonomous vehicle is Tesla's self-driving car.

Chatbots

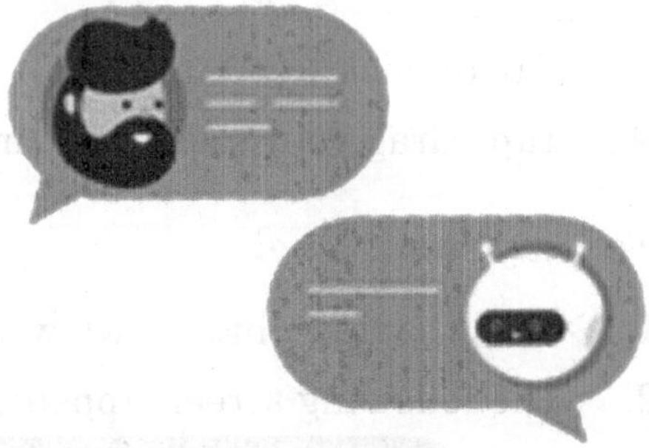

Nowadays Virtual assistants have become a very common technology. Almost every household has a virtual assistant that controls the appliances at home. Example: Siri, Cortana.

Social Media

In social media platforms like Facebook, AI is used for face verification wherein machine learning and deep learning concepts are used to detect facial features and tag your friends.

Tip Bot

AI is all about how the human brain thinks, learn, decides and works to solve a problem.

Activity III

Six Helix

Description

- It a fun game of skill.
- You need to simply turn the helix as the ball jumps. Move down as many levels as possible while avoiding the red colored portions to earn your best score!

Instruction

- Tap or click PLAY to start.
- Tap / drag your mouse to turn the helix as the ball bounces

To Play the Game:

1. Visit the link: https://www.safekidgames.com/six-helix/
2. The following screen appear:

3. Click on Play Button.
4. The following screen appears:

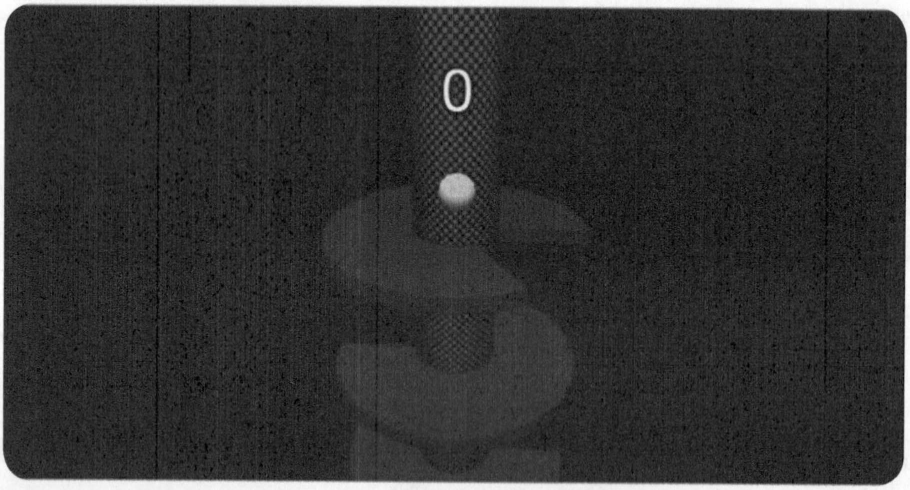

5. Now, move the helix with the help of mouse, as the ball is bouncing move it to the empty space, to let it move to the next helix.

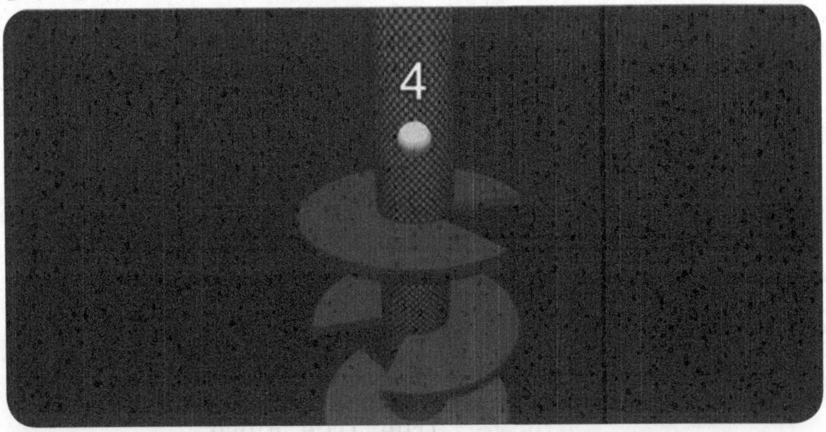

6. You need to avoid the red area on the helix, as when ball stuck on the red surface, the game is over.

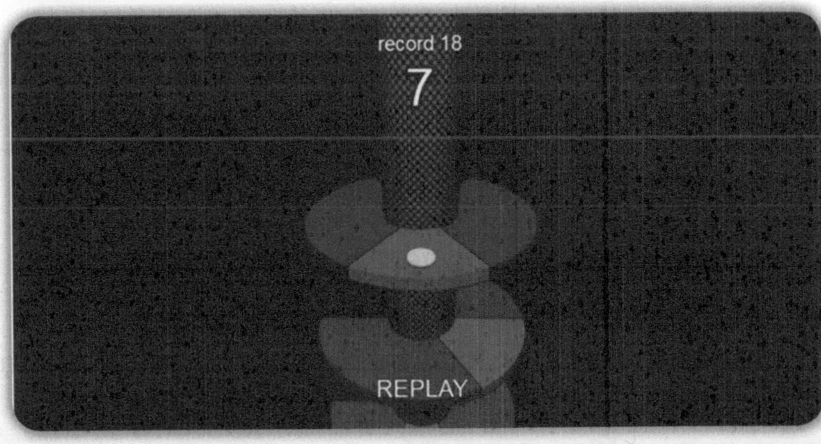

Advantages and Disadvantages of Artificial Intelligence

Advantages	Disadvantages
Reduction in Human Error	High Costs of Creation
Takes risks instead of Humans	Making Humans Lazy
Available 24x7	Leads to Unemployment
Helping in Repetitive Jobs	No Emotions

Memory Bot

Idea behind the introduction of AI is to create technology which allows computers and machines to function in an intelligent manner with or without human supervision.

Check your Progress - I

State whether the following statements are True or False.

a. Artificial Intelligence helps to reduce the human error. True/False

b. Artificial intelligence is available 24x7. True/False

c. AI Robot has emotions? True/False

Answer: True, True, False.

Activity IV

Geo Jump

Description

- This game is challenging and addicting geometry game.
- Game will test your skills as you jump through this exciting adventure of spikes, triangles, rectangles.

Instruction

- Tap or click the geometric character to choose your avatar.
- Tap or click the arrow to play.
- Select your level.
- Tap or click to jump.
- The objective of the game is to follow the rhythm and jump over obstacles.

To play the game:

1. Visit the link: https://www.safekidgames.com/geo-jump/.
2. The following screen appears:

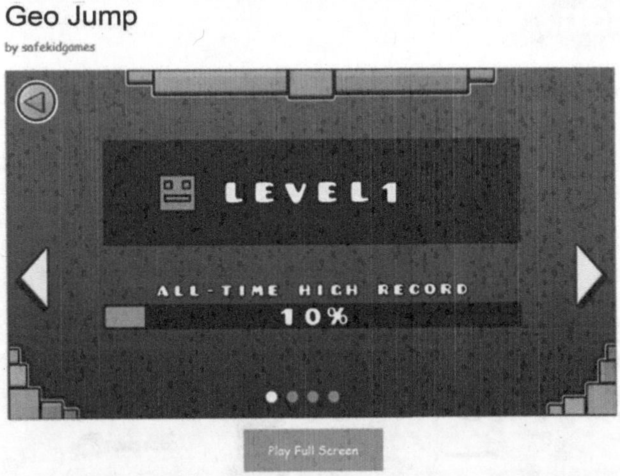

3. Choose your level, in this we have chosen LEVEL 1; and click on LEVEL 1 to start the game.

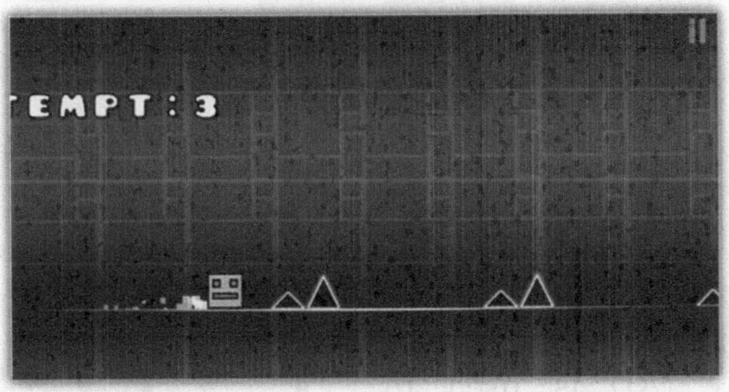

Check your Progress - II

Fill in the Blanks.

Hints: resources, profit, customer

a Banks use AI-based systems to provide ________ support, detect anomalies and credit card frauds.

b Financial organizations are turning to AI to improve their stock trading performance and boost________.

c AI can help farmers to get more from the land while using ________ more sustainably.

Answer: customer, profit, resources.

Gamification

Gamification is the process of adding game-like components to a task to encourage the user participation.

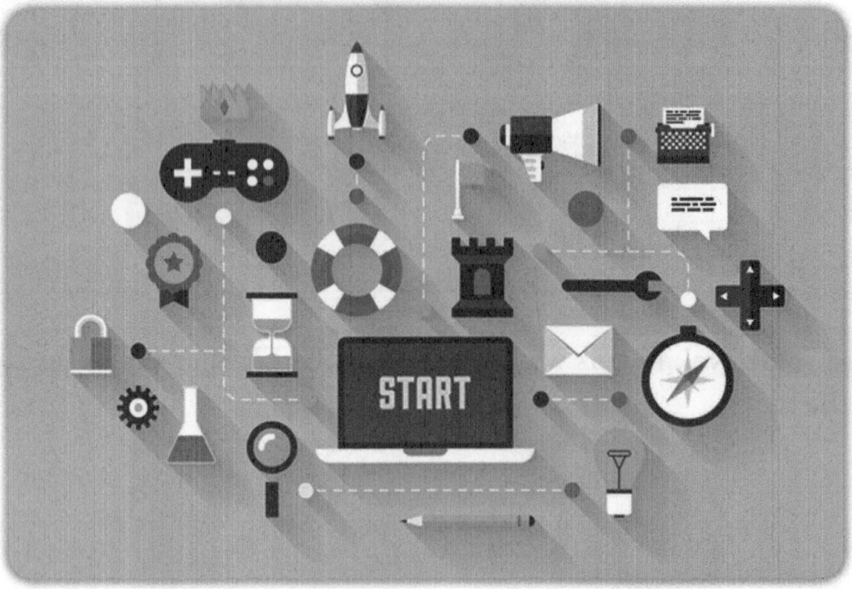

How is Artificial Intelligence used in Games?

Artificial Intelligence (AI) is used to generate responsive, adaptive or intelligent behaviours primarily in Non-Player Characters (NPCs) similar to human-like intelligence.

Gaming actually creates the atmosphere that inspires learners to develop skills and build an emotional connect with the subject.

DEFINITION

Gamification is set of activities and processes to solve problems by applying the characteristics of game elements.

Advantages and Disadvantages of Gamification

Advantages	Disadvantages
Increase learner engagement	High cost of development
Provide instant feedback	Diminished value over time
Boost motivation with features such as Badges	Games are only poorly masked quizzes

Fact Bot

Websites use artificial intelligence to improve the user experience.

Activity V

Pattern Memory Game

Description

- It's a fun game of remembrance of patterns.
- In this you need to remember the pattern of block present to you and then you need to draw the same pattern to move to the next level.

Instruction

- You need to flip the blocks to show the original pattern shown to you.

To play the game:

1. Go to the link: https://www.proprofsgames.com/pattern-memory/
2. The following Page appears:
3. Click on START.

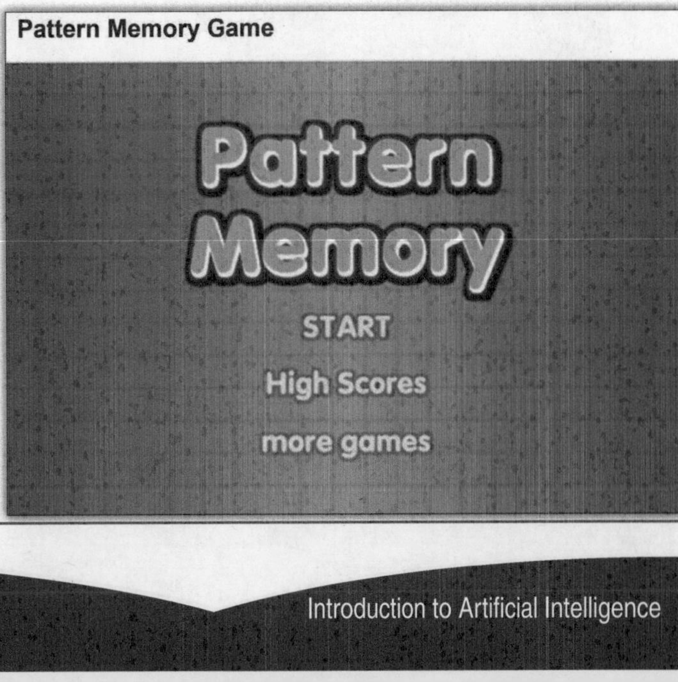

4. The screen with cube appears, which shows the pattern to draw:

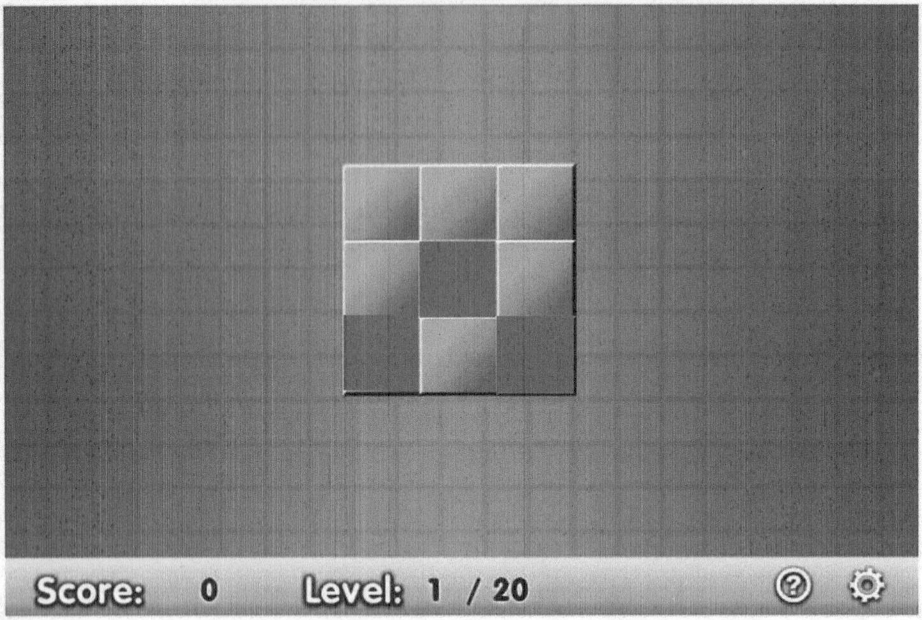

5. The patter get disappears within a second and the following screen appears:

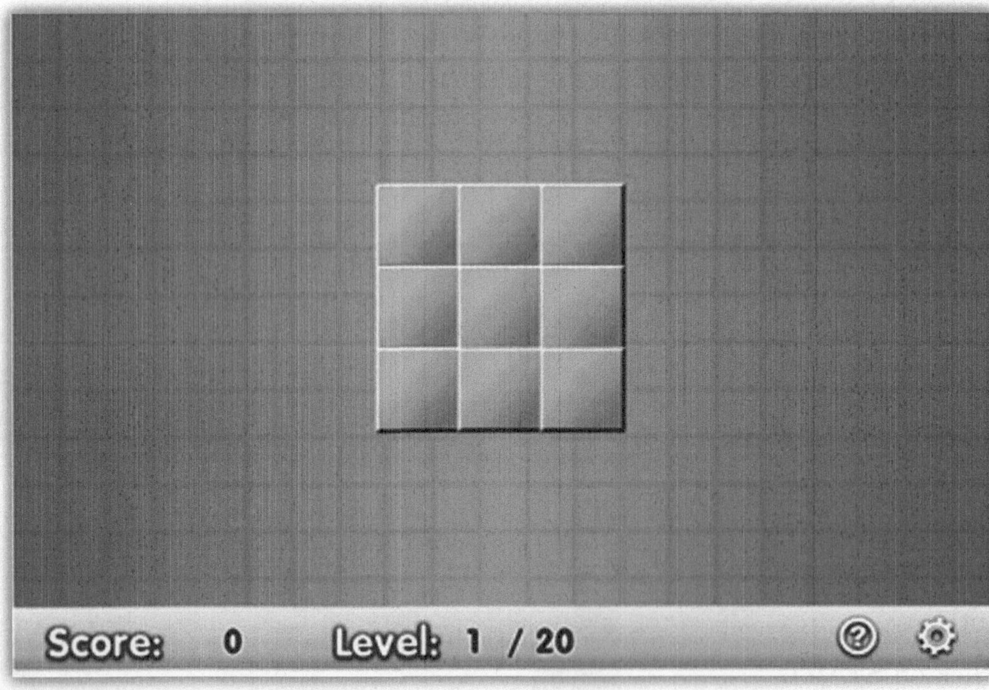

6. Now draw the pattern and move to the next level.

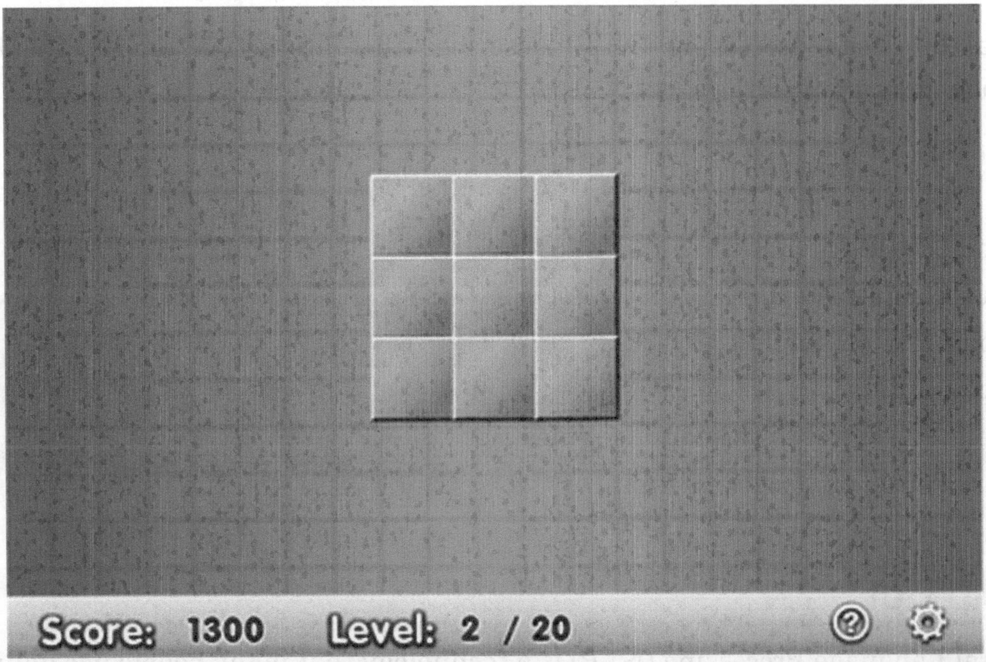

7. In case if you have drawn the incorrect pattern, then the game gets over.

Natural Language Processing (NLP)

Natural language processing (NLP) describes the interaction among the human language and computers.

Examples of NLP that people use every day are:

- Spell check
- Autocomplete text
- Voice text messaging
- Spam filters
- Related keywords on search engines
- Siri, Alexa, or Google Assistant

Tip Bot

Natural Language Processing (NLP) is a technology that many people use daily and has been around for years.

Computer Vision

Computer vision is an interdisciplinary field that deals with how computers can be made to gain high-level understanding from digital images or videos. It seeks to automate tasks that the human visual system can do.

Applications of Computer Vision

- Player Tracking in games
- Cancer Detection
- Finding out the defects in Agriculture
- Plant Recognition
- Autonomous Driving / Self-driving cars

Memory Bot

Computer vision is concerned with the automatic extraction, analysis and understanding of useful information from images.

Check your Progress - III

Tick the correct option.

a Artificial Intelligence (AI) is used to generate **responsive/non-responsive** game.

b Gaming creates the atmosphere that inspires learners to **develop/not to develop** skills.

c Computer vision is concerned with the automatic **extraction/de-extraction**, analysis and understanding of useful information from images.

Answer: responsive, develop, extraction.

Activity VI

Recycle Now

Description

- Game is to recycle what we can and make this world a beautiful place!
- In this game, practice your recycling skills.
- As the recyclable items fall, choose the corresponding box to place the item

Instruction

- Tap or click PLAY to begin.
- As the items appear in the box, drag the item to its respective dustbin.

To play the game:

1. Go to the following link https://www.safekidgames.com/recycling-time/
2. The following screen appears:

3. Click on START button.
4. Select your mode of playing, we have chosen Fun mode

5. The object to recycle will appear in the red rectangular box. Simply drag that object to one of the given dustbin.

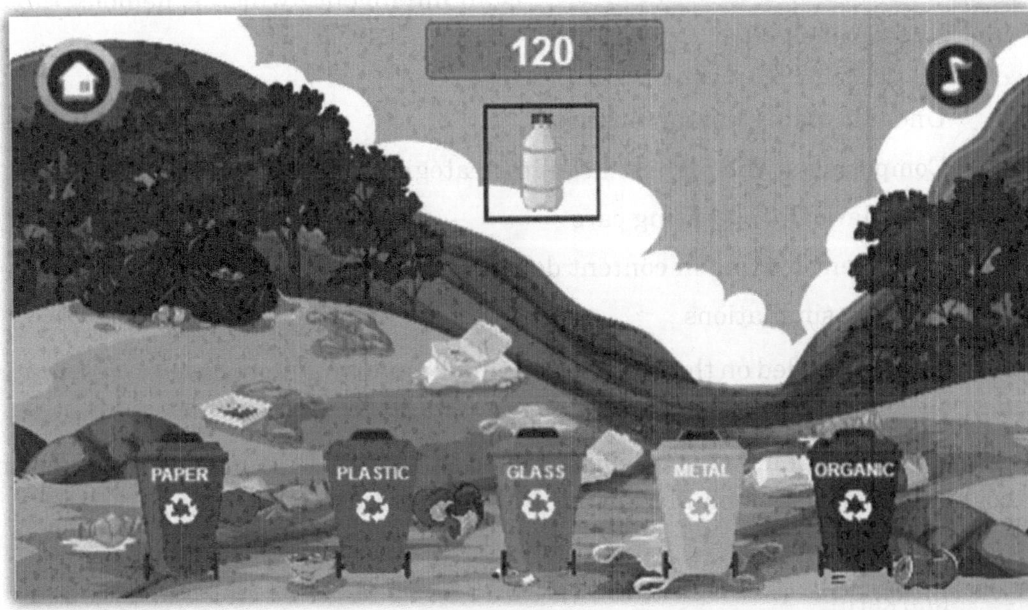

6. Your points will get updated in the blue box.

TECH BOT

- **Artificial intelligence (AI):** Intelligence demonstrated by machines.
- **Autonomous Vehicles/ Self driving cars/ Driverless cars:** Cars that collects data from the vehicles radar, cameras, GPS, and cloud services to produce control signals that operate the vehicle.
- **Chatbots:** Virtual assistant that controls the appliances at home.
  Example: Siri, Cortana.

Recap Bot

- **Artificial intelligence (AI)** is an intelligence which is demonstrated by machines.
- Modern machine capabilities explain that AI include in:
  - Understanding human speech
  - Competing at the highest level in strategic game systems (chess)
  - Automatically operating cars
  - Intelligent routing in content delivery networks
  - Military simulations
- AI field was founded on the assumption that human intelligence "*can be so precisely described that a machine can be made to simulate it*".
- Artificial Intelligence (AI) was first coined in 1956 at Dartmouth Conference by a cognitive scientist, John McCarthy, at the Dartmouth Conference.
- **Applications of AI**
  - Marketing
  - Banking
  - Finance
  - Agriculture
  - Health Care
  - Space Exploration
  - Autonomous Vehicles/ Self driving cars/ Driverless cars
  - Chatbots
  - Social Media
- Gamification is the process of adding game-like components to a task to encourage the participation of user participation.
- Natural language processing (NLP) describes the interaction among the human language and computers.
- Computer vision is an interdisciplinary field that deals with how computers can be made to gain high-level understanding from digital images or videos. It seeks to automate tasks that the human visual system can do.

Brain Bot

A. MULTIPLE CHOICE QUESTIONS.

1. Artificial intelligence (AI) is an intelligence which is demonstrated by:
   a. Machines ☐ b. Humans ☐
   c. Animals ☐ d. Pets ☐
2. AI include in:
   a. Understanding human speech ☐
   b. Competing at the highest level in strategic game systems (chess) ☐
   c. Automatically operating cars ☐
   d. All of the above ☐
3. Artificial Intelligence is when a computer program or machine can think and learn.
   a. Move ☐ b. Learn ☐
   c. Teach ☐ d. know ☐
4. AI field was founded on the assumption that human intelligence "can be so precisely described that a machine can be made to ________ it".
   a. Simulate ☐ b. Learn ☐
   c. Think ☐ d. Teach ☐
5. Artificial intelligence (AI) refers to the simulation of human intelligence in the machines which are programmed to think and mimic the actions of ______.
   a. Machines ☐ b. Humans ☐
   c. Animals ☐ d. Pets ☐

B. FILL IN THE BLANKS.

Hint: facial, self-driving, verification virtual, face, kepler

1. Astronomers used Artificial Intelligence to sift through years of data obtained by the ________ telescope in order to identify a distant eight-planet solar system.
2. ________ cars have been a buzzword in the AI industry.

3. Almost every household has a ________ assistant that controls the appliances at home.
4. In social media platforms like Facebook, AI is used for ________ .
5. Machine learning and deep learning concepts are used to detect ________ features and tag your friends.

C. MATCH THE FOLLOWING.

Column A	Column B
1. Marketing	i. AI can help farmers to use resources more sustainably
2. Banking	ii. AI-based systems to provide customer support
3. Finance	iii. AI algorithm or a bot for marketing a brand or a company
4. Agriculture	iv. Digitalized device that can find cardiac diseases
5. Health Care	v. AI to improve the stock trading performance and boost profit.

D. ANSWER THE FOLLOWING QUESTIONS.

1. Define the term Artificial Intelligence.

____

____

____

2. Name any two applications of Artificial Intelligence.

____

____

____

3. What is Gamification.

____

____

____

4. What do you mean by Natural Language Processing?

____

____

____

5. Define the term Computer Vision.

____

____

____

Lab Activity Math Up

Description

- In this game keep your ball bouncing, and hit the answer and WIN!

Instructions

- Click to START.
- You need to tap quickly and keep your ball moving.
- There are multiple answers rotating around the math fact.
- Bounce your ball to the right answer.
- In case, if your ball drops or hits the wrong answer, you're OUT.

To play the game:

1. Visit the link: https://www.safekidgames.com/math-up/
2. The following screen appears:

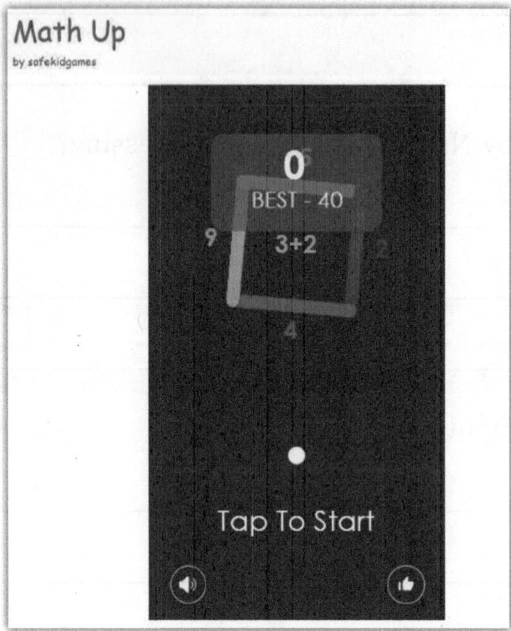

3. Click on Start.
4. Make your ball bounce and hit the answer, after solving the equation given.

WORKSHEET

A. STATE WHETHER THE FOLLOWING STATEMENT ARE TRUE OR FALSE.

1. AI is all about how the human brain thinks, learn, decides and works to solve a problem. True/False
2. AI does not make humans Lazy. True/False
3. AI leads to increase in Unemployment. True/False
4. Idea behind the introduction of AI is to create technology which allows computers and machines to function in an intelligent manner with or without human supervision True/False
5. Virtual assistants have become a very common technology. True/False

B. FILL IN THE BLANKS.

Hints: home attributes, virtual assistant, Cortana, Gamification, speech

1. ___________ control the appliances/gadgets/systems such as TV, AC, fridge, and so on, with your device.
2. Virtual assistant will monitor and/or control the ___________.
3. Computer programs like Siri or Alexa uses smart technology to recognize the ___________ and to respond.
4. Siri and ___________ are virtual assistant.
5. ___________ is the process of adding game-like components to a task to encourage the participation of user participation.

C. ANSWER THE FOLLOWING QUESTIONS.

1. Define the use of AI in social media.

____

____

2. What is the main goal of AI?

3. Name any two applications of Natural language processing.

4. Write any one advantage and disadvantage of AI.

5. Write any one application of Computer Vision.

Quiz Card

TICK THE CORRECT ANSWER.

1. Artificial Intelligence (AI) is used to generate__________ in Non-Player Characters (NPCs) similar to human-like intelligence
   a. Responsive b. adaptive
   c. intelligent behaviours d. All of the above.
2. Gaming actually creates the atmosphere that inspires learners to develop _________and build an emotional connect with the subject.
   a. Intelligence b. Skills
   c. Activity d. Game element
3. Natural language processing (NLP) describes the interaction among the ________ language and computers.
   a. Animals b. Human
   c. Pets d. Robots
4. NLP that people use every day are:
   a. Spell check b. Autocomplete
   c. Voice text messaging d. All of the above
5. Computer vision is an interdisciplinary field that deals with how ________can be made to gain high-level understanding from digital images or videos.
   a. Human b. Robots
   c. Chatbots d. Computers
6. __________ seeks to automate tasks that the human visual system can do.
   a. Gamification b. Natural language processing
   c. Computer vision d. Artificial intelligence
7. Computer Vision can be used in:
   a. Player Tracking in games b. Cancer Detection
   c. Finding defects in Agriculture
   d. All of the above
8. __________ areas can contribute to build an intelligent system.
   a. Philosophy b. Biology
   c. Sociology d. All of the above
9. Which of the following is an application of AI?
   a. Gaming b. Non Expert Systems
   c. Visual Systems d. Non-gaming system
10. ___________is used to adjust the house temperature
   a. Smart Home device b. Smartphone
   c. Smart Car d. Remote control

Notes

2 ARTIFICIAL INTELLIGENCE IN REALITY

Structure Bot

In this chapter, we will discuss:

- The meaning of the term Smart Home
- Applications of Smart Home
- Advantages and Disadvantages of Smart Home

Objective Bot

At the end of this chapter, you should be able to:

- Understand the use of inklewriter
- Interact and create an interactive story using inklewriter add-on around an ultramodern home
- Evaluate the AI skills required for futuristic jobs

Introduction to Smart Home

Smart homes are homes that have all the electronic devices and security systems which are controlled by the owner with the click of button.

In Smart home:

- From ventilation to heating, from security to air conditioning, everything will be in your control, at a distance of a button.
- With a click of button; you can have the entire control of which device would be working and which would stop working, right away.

Home automation or domestics is a building automation for a home, known as smart home or smart house.

Fact Bot

AI, similar to everything in our reality, has its own life cycle.

Activity I

Dream House

Are you Ready to design your dream house?

- In this game, use your imagination to construct the home of your dreams.
- You can add doors, windows, change the colors, layouts, can add landscape, and many more to your home.
- When you're done, take a screenshot and share your masterpiece!

Instruction

- Use the menu on the left to choose which item which you like to use to design your home.
- Click on a menu item to see the available options.
- You can also choose a "day" or "night" landscape present to the right of the screen.
- Once you design the home, save it and share your masterpiece.

To play the game:

1. Go to the link: https://www.safekidgames.com/dream-house/
2. The following screen appear:

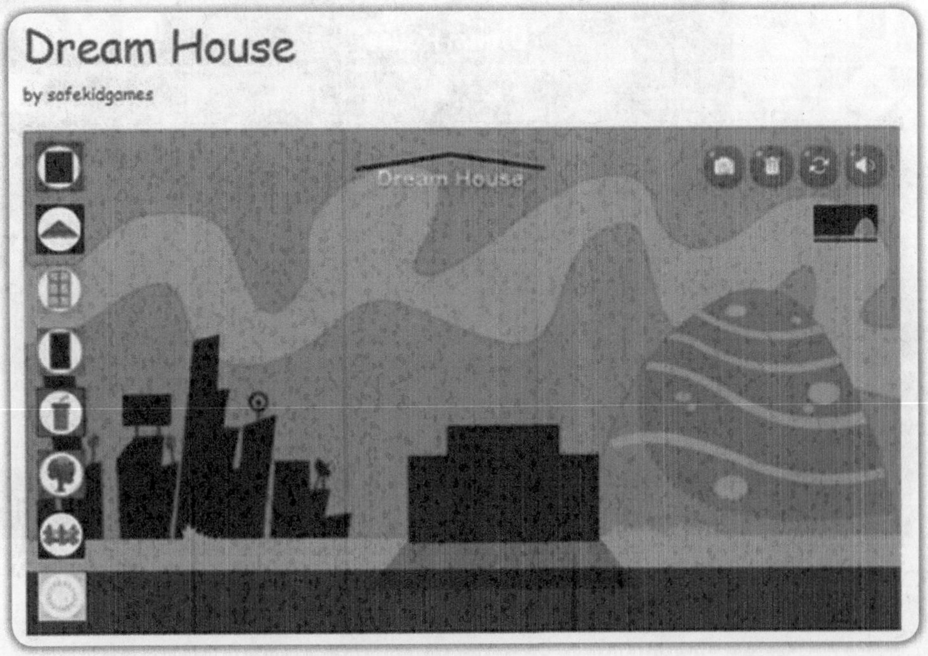

3. Start designing your home..
4. We have changed the landscape mode to night, you can choose the wall design as shown:

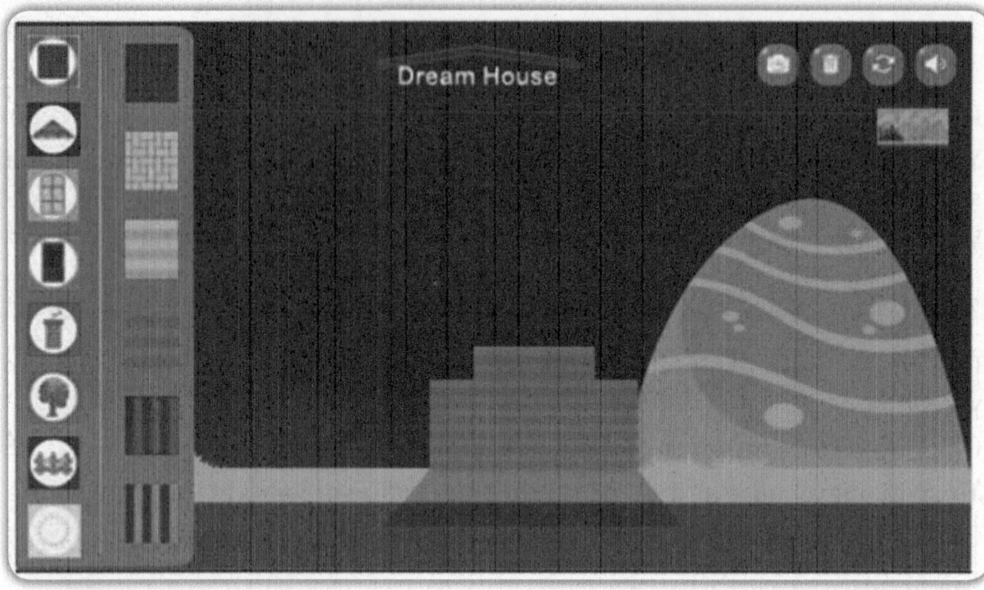

5. Add the roof to your house:

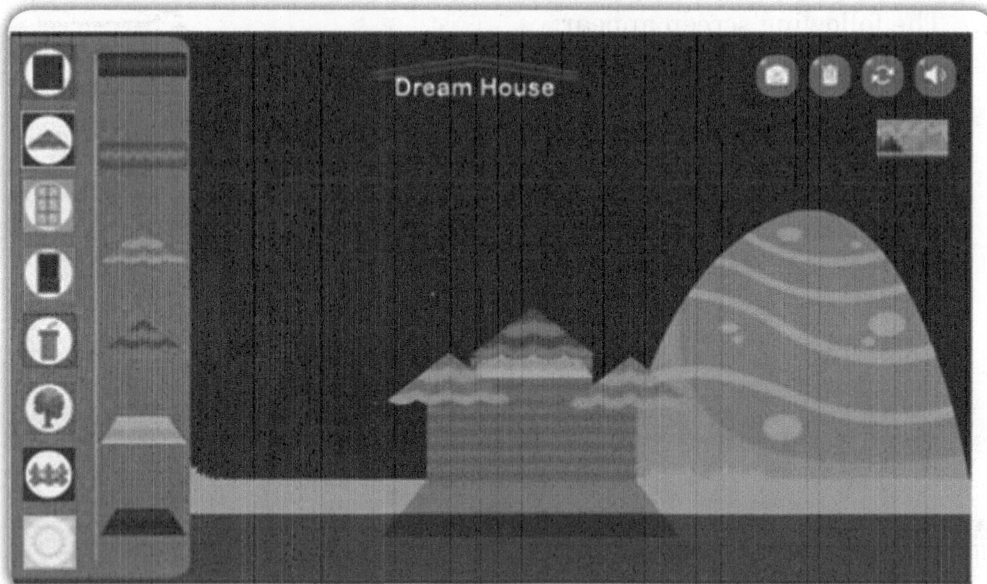

6. Add doors, windows, trees, fence and many more...

A home automation system will:

- Monitor and/or control the home attributes (lighting, climate, entertainment systems)
- Provide security to your home (access control and alarm systems).

DEFINITION

Smart Home is a home that can be managed remotely to control the appliances/ gadgets/systems such as TV, AC, fridge, and so on, with your device.

Activity II

Flip It Game

Description

It is a challenging mind game. In this you have to flip all the pegs to the opposite side. But keep in mind that when you flip a peg, its surrounding pegs will also be flipped

Instruction

- Click on the peg to turn it white.

To play the game:

1. Visit the link: https://www.proprofsgames.com/flip-it/
2. The following screen appear:

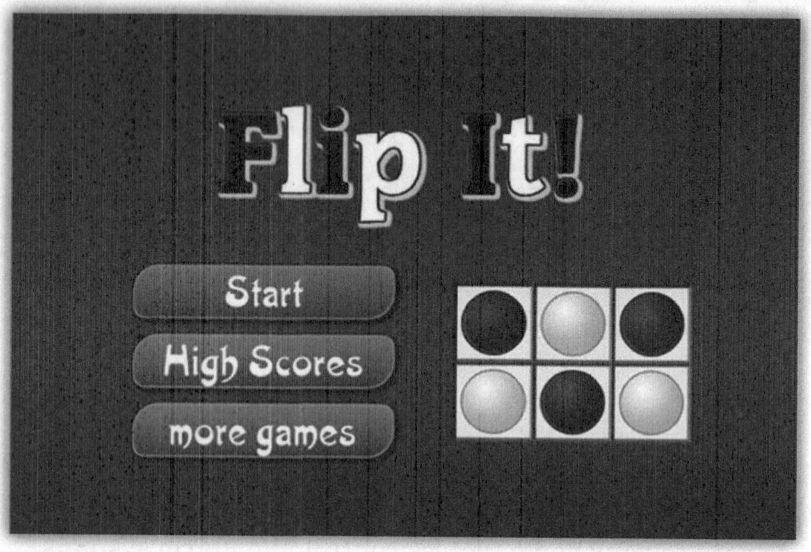

3. Click on START.
4. Click on the peg to make it flip to white.
5. Your moves and score will be displayed on the right side.

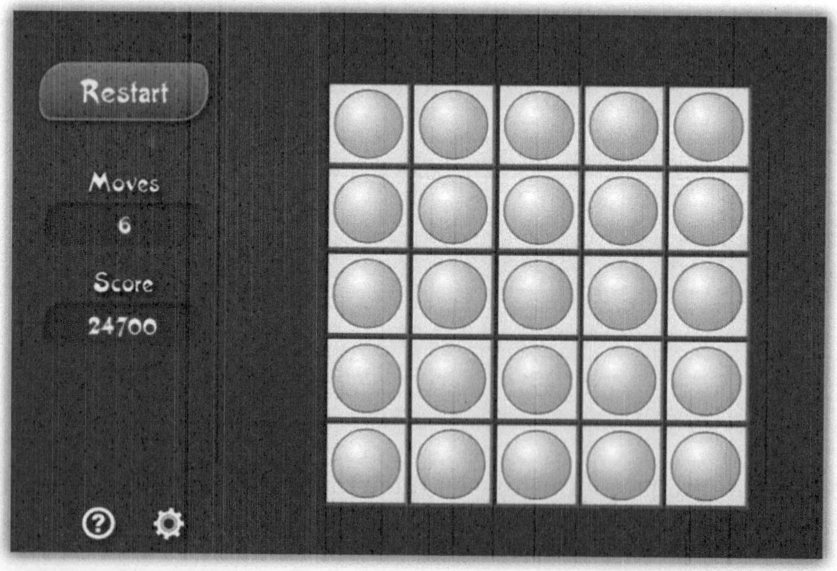

Example of Smart Home technology

Smart TV: Connected to the internet to access on-demand video and music.

Smart lighting: Systems can detect when persons are in the room and adjust lighting as needed.

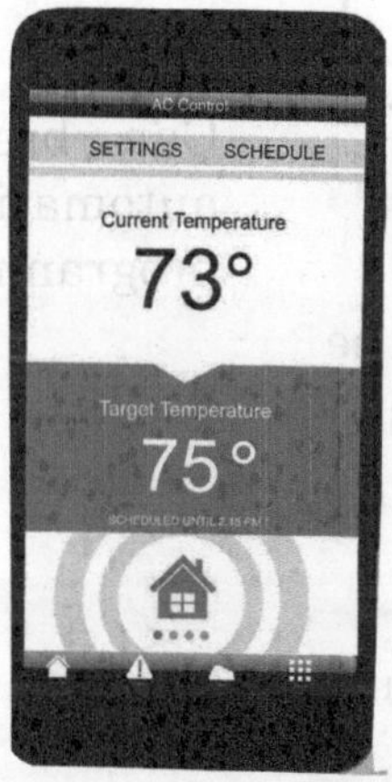

Smart thermostats: Connected with Wi-Fi, allowing users to schedule monitor and remotely control the home temperatures.

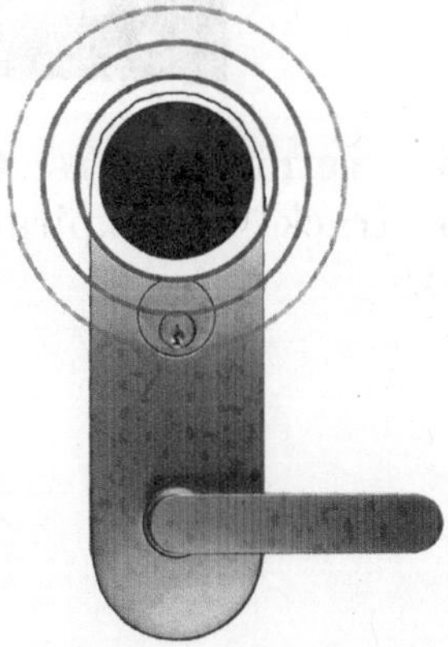

Smart locks and garage-door openers: Can grant or deny access to visitors.

Smart security cameras: You can monitor your homes when you are away or on vacation.

Automated Pet food: It can be automated with connected feeders.

Houseplants and lawns: Can be watered by way of connected timers.

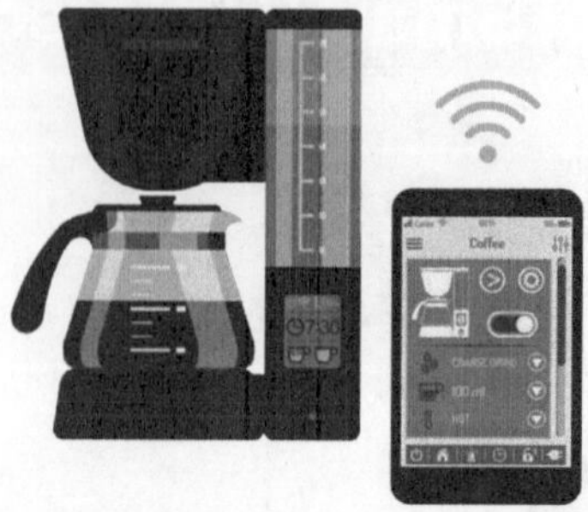

Smart coffee makers: Can brew a fresh cup automatically at a programmed time.

Smart refrigerators: Can keep track of expiration dates.

Tip Bot

Smart security camera/ lock are the most used smart devices.

Activity III

Disc Battle Game

Description

- It is an air hockey game.
- In this you need to compete with the computer to shoot the disc into each other's base.
- Remember, you need to avoid the other side from shooting the disc into your base.
- Both of you will hit the disc by using a round pad so the direction of the disc may not be easily controlled

To play the game:

1. Go to the link: https://www.proprofsgames.com/disc-battle/
2. The following Page appears:

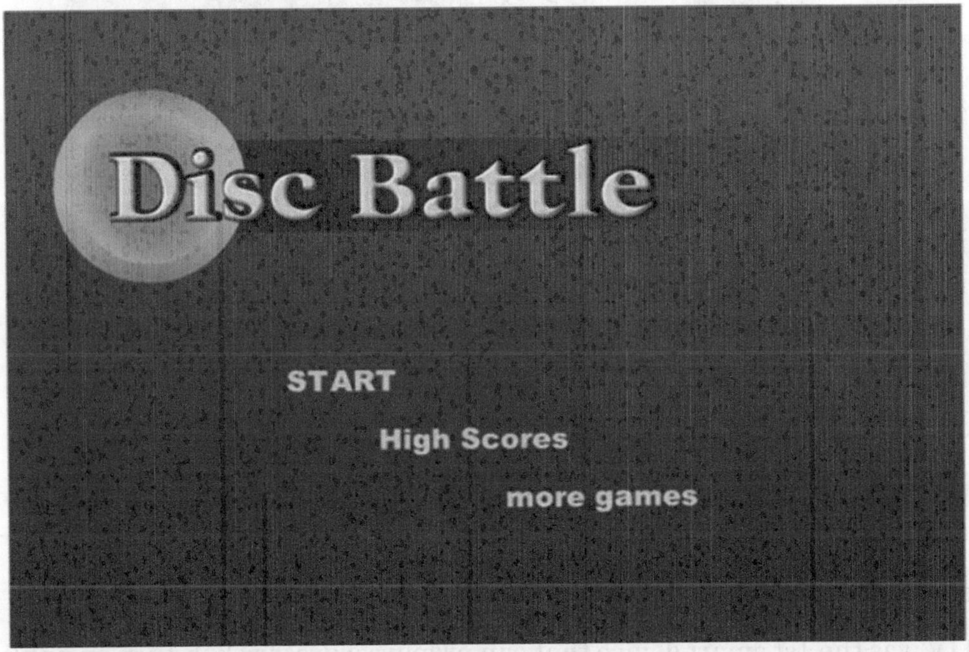

3. Click on START to play the game and the following screen appears:

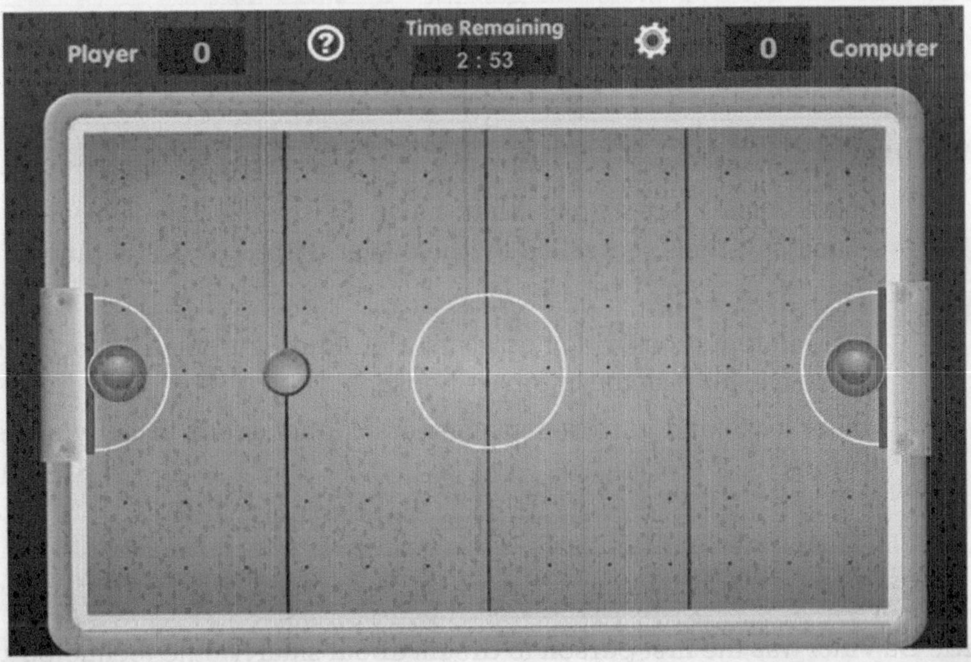

4. Left side is your's and right side is of computer, move the disc to computer's player side to goal.

Memory Bot

ECHO IV was the 1st smart device that can prepare a grocery list, turn on appliances, and control the room temperature; but was never sold commercially.

Check your Progress - I

State whether the following statements are True or False.

a Smart homes are homes that have all the electronic devices and security systems controlled by the owner with the click of button. True/False

b Home automation or domestics is a building automation for a home, known as smart home or smart house. True/False

c Smart locks and garage-door openers cannot grant or deny access to visitors. True/False

Answer: True, True, False.

Fact Bot

Leonardo Da Vinci was the first person to dream about smart home technology.

Application of Smart Home/Home Automation

Heating, ventilation and air conditioning (HVAC)

Home robots and security

Smart Grid and a smart meter, to run washing machines

Lighting control system

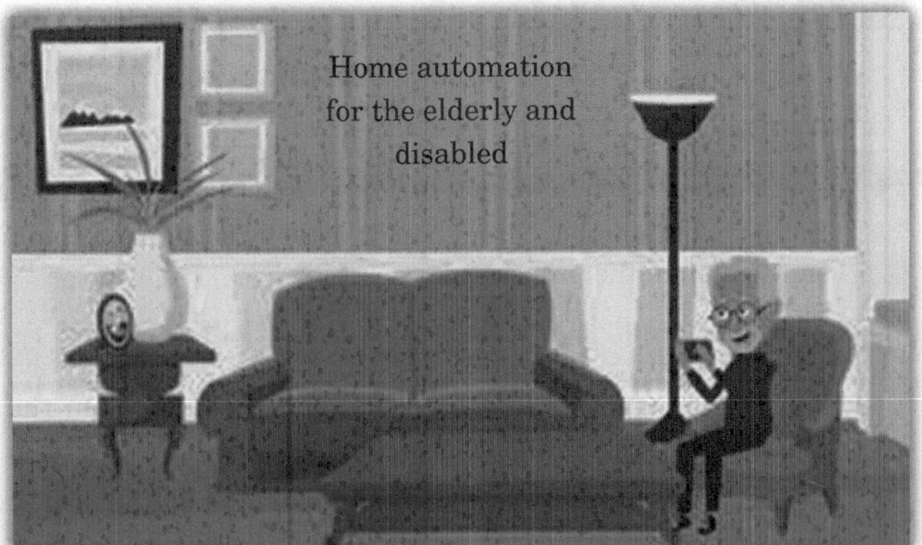

Home automation for the elderly and disabled

Tip Bot

Smart Home technology can help you to reduce the amount of electricity wasted in the household.

Advantages and Disadvantages of Smart Home / Home Automation

Advantages	Disadvantages
Energy Efficient	High Cost
Hands-free convenience	Internet Dependency
Enhanced Security	Need more setup and configuration
Save Time with Automated Tasks	More Technical Security Threats

Memory Bot

Home automation or domestics is a building automation for a home, known as smart home or smart house.

Activity IV

Robot Island

Description

- It is a game which helps you to learn the basic programming skills.
- In this help the robot through each level by selecting a command and placing it on the map in the proper order.

Instruction

- Tap the command button to select, and then tap it on the floor to place the command button on the floor to guide the robot the direction.
- In case if you have placed the wrong command on the floor, tap the command to delete it.
- To delete all the commands tap the CLEAR[X] button.
- To play tap GO.

To play the game:

1. Visit the link: https://www.abcya.com/games/robot_islands
2. The following screen appears:

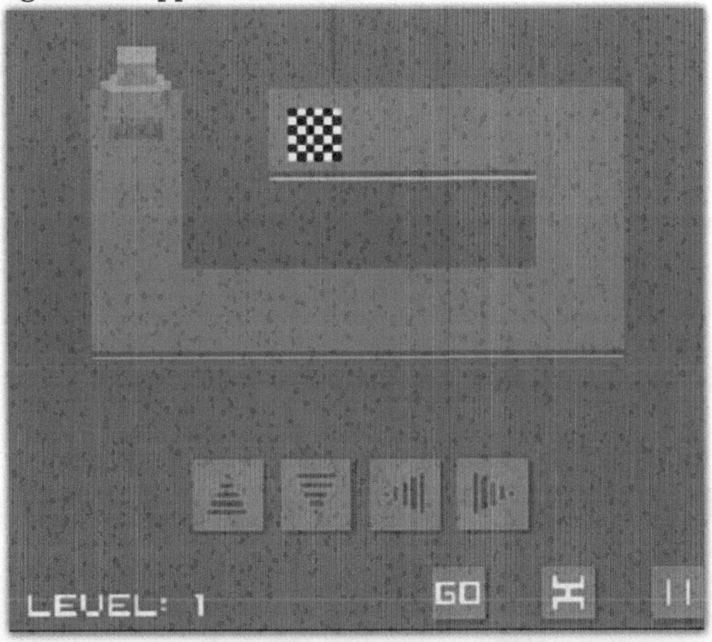

3. Place the arrows as shown below, and help the robot to complete the race.

4. Press Go, robot will follow the path and reach its destination.

Check your Progress - II

Fill in the Blanks.

Hints: attributes, high, smart home

a. A home automation system will monitor and/or control the home ___________ (lighting, climate, entertainment systems).

b. Home automation or domestics is a building automation for a home, known as ___________ or smart house.

c. To make your home a smart home will incur a ___________ cost.

Answer: attributes, smart home, high

inklewriter

inklewriter will help writers to tell interactive tales with the minimum of fuss. It will help you to write story in an organised manner, and to concentrate only on the writing.

It's a freely available tool designed to allow anyone to write and publish interactive stories. It is helpful for both teachers and students who are looking to mix computer skills and creative writing.

To start writing on inklewriter:

1. Click on the link: https://www.inklestudios.com/inklewriter/
2. The following screen of inklewriter appears:

3. Click on Start Writing.

4. A page appears displaying a message as Inklewriter has been reborn!

<u>The new version of inklewriter is now at inklewriter.com.</u>

5. Click on inklewriter.com
6. The following screen appears:

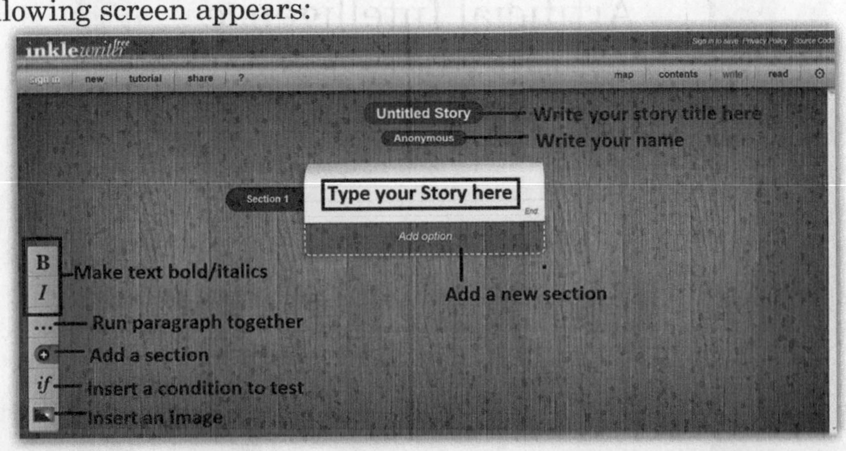

7. When you completed typing the text.

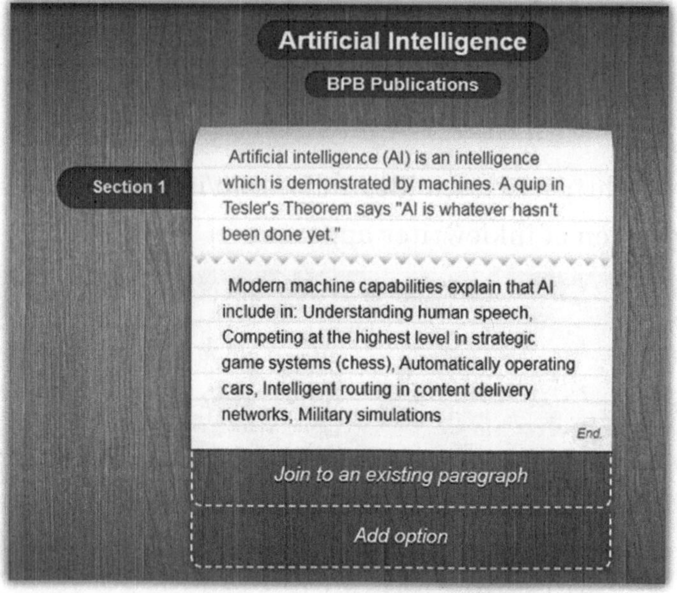

8. Click on read button.

9. The following screen appears showing the final outcome of the writing.

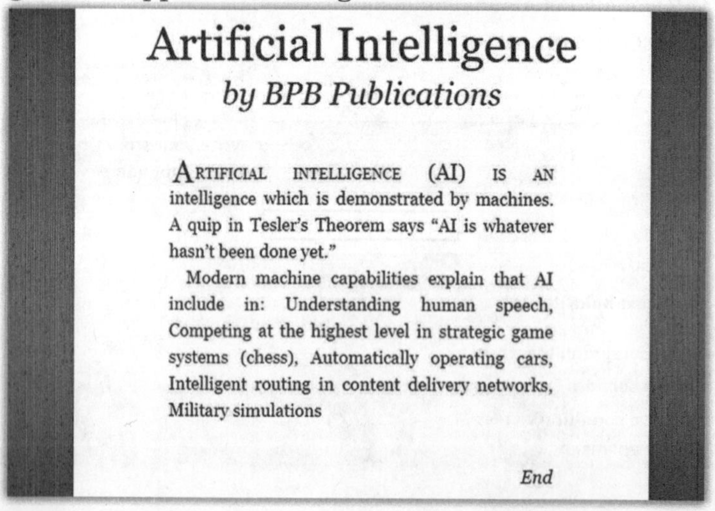

10. To share your story, click on:

DEFINITION

inklewriter will help writers to tell interactive tales with the minimum of fuss.

See the interactive tale in inklewriter

1. Visit the link: https://oldinklewriter.inklestudios.com/stories/9mxn
2. The following screen appears:

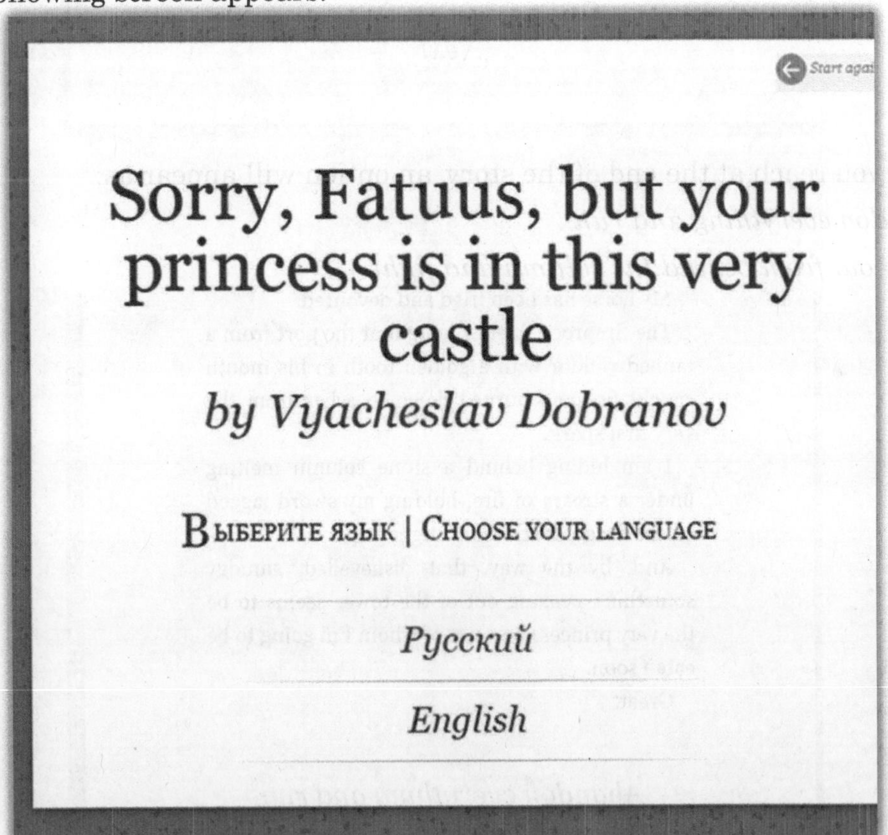

3. Choose language: English.
4. The story appears, you can now read the story and to read the next section click on next.

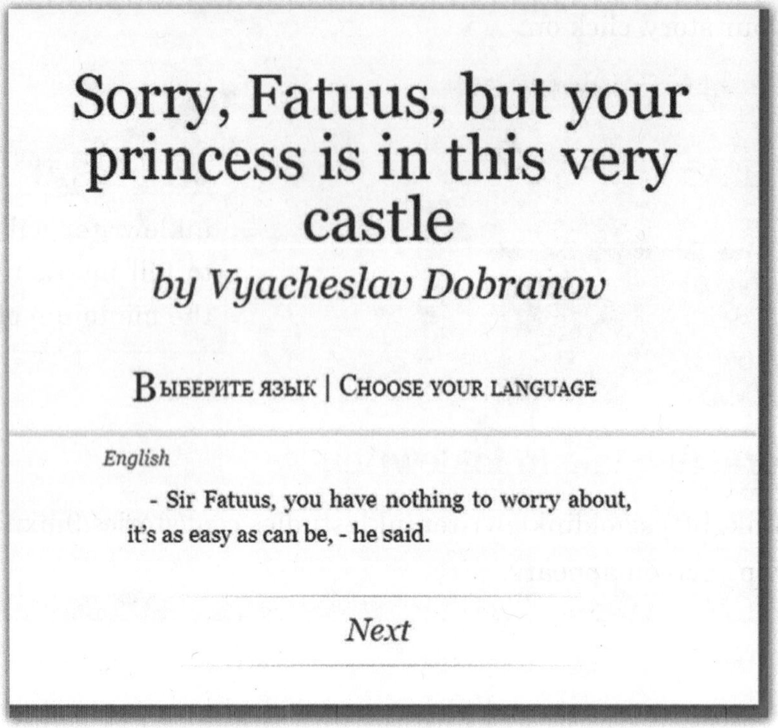

5. Once you reach at the end of the story, an option will appear as:
   Abandon everything and run
   Jump out from behind the column and fight

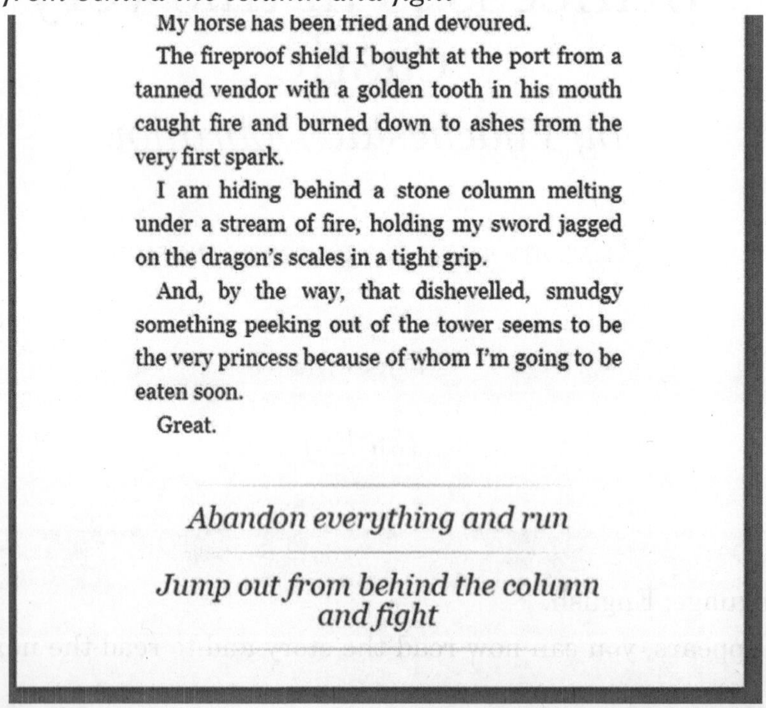

6. Choose the option as per your choice. In this case we have chosen Abandon everything and run; and after this an conclusion note appears; and the story ends.
7. In case if you choose: Jump out from behind the column and fight; then a different aspect of story will appears and you can select the option as provided further and continue to read the story.

Great.

Jump out from behind the column and fight

"What do you think you're doing, idiot?" I think to myself as I jump out with a wild cry before the dragon at the very moment he finally stops pouring liquid fire all over my hideout, and starts filling his mighty lungs with air.

Whistling is the air in the dragon's long neck is... Glittering are the scales on his broad chest... Glaring are his red eyes under the long spikes on his head... Pounding are his muscular feet on the floor...

Trembling with fear is my pathetic body.

Throw the sword at the dragon's eye

Run under the dragon

Activity V

Math Line

Description

- It's a fun game of Maths.
- Destroy the balls by forming pairs that add up to 10.
- You can use one ball to destroy a group of same numbered balls.

To play the game:

1. Go to the link: https://www.proprofsgames.com/math-lines/
2. The following Page appears:

3. Click on START.
4. Shoot the ball to the number which adds up to 10.

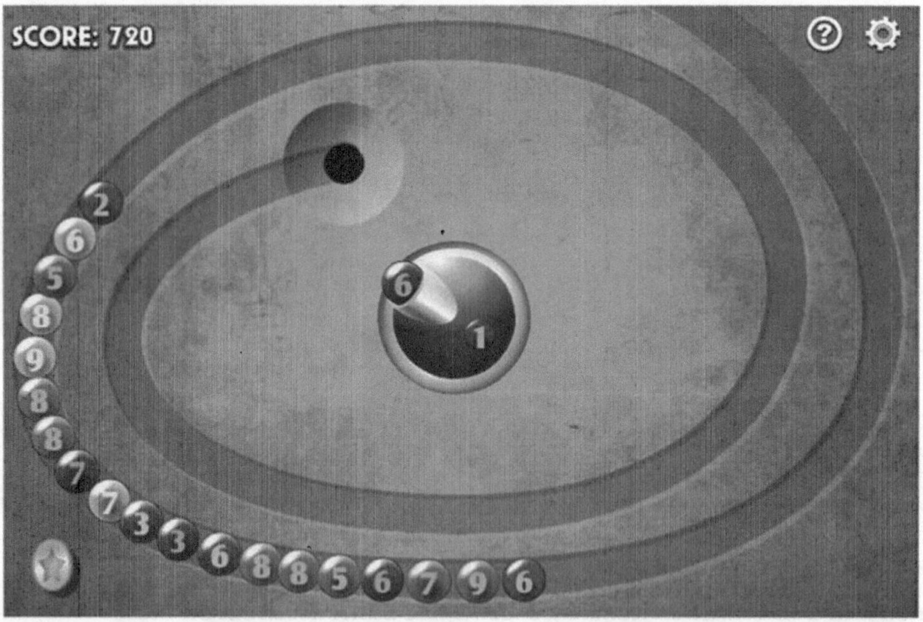

Fact Bot

inklewriter is a open source, that means any one can use this.

Activity VI

Connect Four Game

Description

- It's a classic strategy game in which you have to Connect Four balls.
- In this game you and the computer take turns one by one to put down coloured pegs, once the peg of a colour forms a line of 4, the game is won.

To play the game:

1. Go to the following link https://www.proprofsgames.com/connect-four/
2. The following screen appears:

3. Click on START button.
4. Following screen appear:

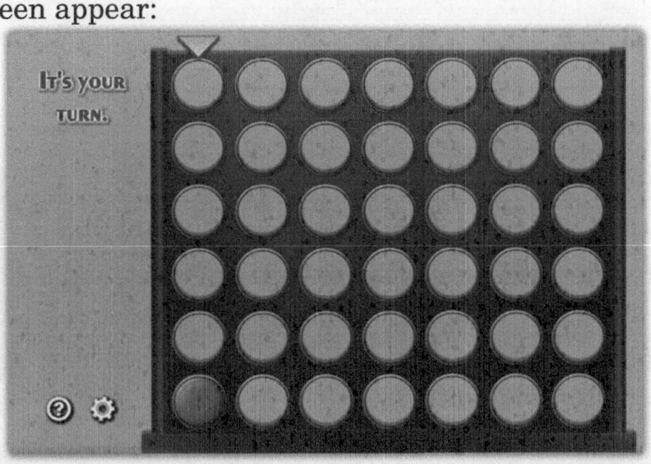

5. Make four balls in a line to win the game.

Tip Bot

Smart Device: Echo Dot Kids Edition

- Echo Dot Kids Edition lets kid get in on the fun.
- It's a voice-controlled gadget that has a bright rainbow design, and it's equipped with kid-friendly skills (playing music, telling stories and calling friends and family members).
- Parents can set daily time limits and can also review activity on the device.

Check your Progress - III

Tick the correct option.

a An inklewriter will help writers to tell interactive tales with the **minimum / maximum** of fuss.

b inklewriter will help you to write story in an **organised/non-organised** manner, and to concentrate only on the writing.

c inklewriter is a freely available tool designed to allow anyone to write and publish **interactive/non-interactive** stories.

Answer: minimum, organised, interactive.

Memory Bot

Fitbit Ace 2 Activity Tracker for Kids

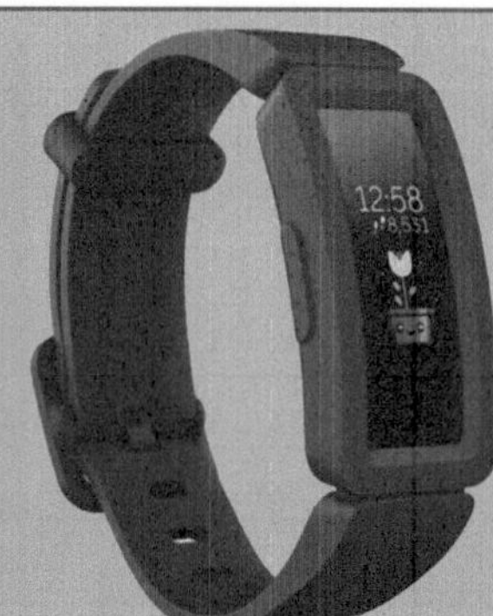

- Its' a fitness tracker designed for kids of age six and up.
- Its a bracelet-style tracker which is worn on wrist and can monitors steps, active minutes and sleep habits.
- Device can also synchronize with Fitbit app, where parents can monitor kids' activity.

TECH BOT

- **Smart Home:** Home that can be managed remotely to control the appliances/ gadgets/systems such as TV, AC, fridge, and so on, with your device.
- **Smart TV:** TV connected to the internet to access on-demand video and music.
- **Smart lighting systems:** Devices which can detect when persons are in the room and adjust lighting as needed.

Recap Bot

- Smart homes are homes that have all the electronic devices and security systems which are controlled by the owner with the click of button.
- Home automation or domestics is a building automation for a home, known as smart home or smart house.
- Example of Smart Home technology:
  - Smart TV
  - Smart lighting systems
  - Smart thermostats
  - Smart locks and garage-door openers
  - Smart security cameras
  - Pet care can be automated with connected feeders
  - Houseplants and lawns can be watered by way of connected timers
  - Smart coffee makers can brew a fresh cup automatically at a programmed time
  - Smart refrigerators can keep track of expiration dates
- Application of Smart Home/ Home Automation:
  - Heating, ventilation and air conditioning (HVAC)
  - Lighting control system
  - Smart Grid and a smart meter, to run washing machines
  - Home robots and security
  - Home automation for the elderly and disabled
- inklewriter will help writers to tell interactive tales with the minimum of fuss. It will help you to write story in an organised manner, and to concentrate only on the writing.

Brain Bot

A. MULTIPLE CHOICE QUESTIONS.

1. Smart homes are homes that have all the electronic devices and security systems which are controlled by the owner with the click of:

   a Button ☐ b TV ☐

   c Light ☐ d Camera ☐

2. AI, similar to everything in our reality, has its own ____ cycle.

   a Camera ☐ b Life ☐

   c Monitor ☐ d Security ☐

3. A home automation system will:

   a Monitor and/or control the home attributes ☐

   b Access control and alarm systems ☐

   c Both a and b ☐

   d None of the above ☐

4. Smart Home is a home that can be managed remotely to control the appliances/gadgets/systems such as TV, AC, fridge, and so on, with your:

   a Hand ☐ b Presence ☐

   c Device ☐ d Pets ☐

5. Smart TV are connected to the internet to access on-demand:

   a Video ☐ b Music ☐

   c Both a and b ☐ d None of the above ☐

B. FILL IN THE BLANKS.

Hints: button, control, smart home, home attributes, lighting

1. From ventilation to heating, from security to air conditioning, everything will be in your control, at a distance of a __________.
2. You click a button and you can have the entire __________ of which device would be working and which would stop working, right away.
3. Home automation or domestics is a building automation for a home, known as __________ or smart house.
4. A home automation system will monitor and/or control the __________.

5. Smart lighting systems can detect when persons are in the room and adjust ____________ as needed.

C. MATCH THE FOLLOWING.

Column A	Column B
1. Smart thermostats	i. monitor your homes when you are away or on vacation
2. Smart locks and garage-door openers	ii. automated connected feeders
3. Smart security cameras	iii. watered by way of connected timers
4. Pet care	iv. remotely control the home temperatures
5. Houseplants	v. grant or deny access to visitors

D. ANSWER THE FOLLOWING QUESTIONS.

1. Define the term Smart home.

____

____

____

2. Name any two applications of Smart home.

____

____

____

3. What is inklewriter?

____

____

____

4. What do you mean by Smart TV?

____

____

____

5. Define the term Smart refrigerator.

____

____

____

Lab Activity The Eight Queens Game

Description

- In this game you have to place all the eight queens on the chess board, but not in the same direction/row/column/horizontally or vertically.

Instructions

- The objective of this game is to put all the 8 queens onto the chess board without the queens capturing each other.

To play the game:

1. Visit the link: https://www.proprofsgames.com/the-eight-queens/
2. The following screen appears:

3. Click on START.
4. Chess board appears, all the queen are present on the right side of the board, the number of queens put on the board will appear on the left side at "Queens Put", your time will be recorded.

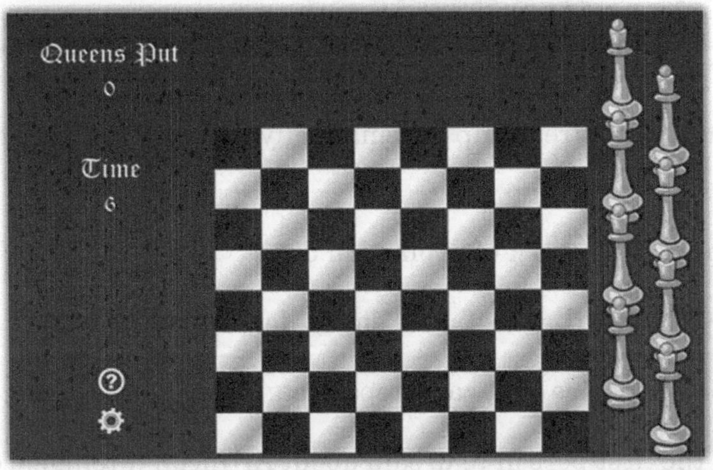

5. Start placing the queens on the board.

6. Once you are done, you can also play again the game.

WORKSHEET

A. STATE WHETHER THE FOLLOWING STATEMENT ARE TRUE OR FALSE.

1. Smart coffee makers can brew a fresh cup automatically at a programmed time. True/False

2. Smart refrigerators cannot keep track of expiration dates. True/False

3. Smart security camera/ lock are the most used smart devices. True/False

4. ECHO IV was the 1st smart device that can prepare a grocery list. True/False

5. Leonardo Da Vinci was the first person to dream about Artificial intelligence. True/False

B. FILL IN THE BLANKS.

Hints: thermostats, locks, security cameras, Pet care, Houseplants

1. Smart ___________ remotely control the home temperatures.

2. Smart ___________ and garage-door openers can grant or deny access to visitors.

3. Smart ___________ through which you can monitor your homes when you away or on vacation.

4. ___________ can be automated with connected feeders.

5. ___________ and lawns can be watered by way of connected timers.

C. ANSWER THE FOLLOWING QUESTIONS.

1. Write the use of SmartHomes.

____

____

____

2. What is the main goal of inklewriter?

3. Write any one advantage and disadvantage of Smart home.

4. Define the use of smart lighting system.

5. Explain how Smart coffee makers are helpful.

Quiz Card

TICK THE CORRECT ANSWER.

1. Another term for a smart home is:

   a Future Home b Home Automation

   c Sci-fi Home d Robotic Home

2. Smart home technology was first introduced in:

   a 1974 b 1975

   c 1976 d 1977

3. _______ can be used to remotely control your security system.

   a Smart Phone b Tablet

   c Computer d All of the above

4. Is solar panels can be used in conjunction with smart home products?

   a True b False

5. Most smart home systems are only geared towards a younger audience.

   a True b False

6. ________ is the average amount spent on energy costs for a single smart home every year.

   a ₹ 100000/- b ₹ 200000/-

   c ₹ 300000/- d ₹ 400000/-

7. Smart energy efficient products can qualify you for tax incentives.

   a True b False

8. __________is the product that users wish to control with home automation.

   a Central Heating b Washer/Dryer

   c Lights d Kitchen Appliances

9. ___________ is a feature of most smart thermostats.

   a Programmable schedules b Energy savings on a yearly basis

   c Digital displays d All of the above

10. You can ___________ remotely with smart home technology?

    a Read with your kids a bedtime story

    b Check to see if you left the television ON

    c Turn ON the shower

    d Open and close your windows

Notes

Notes

3 SUSTAINABLE DEVELOPMENT GOALS

Structure Bot

In this chapter, we will discuss:

- Sustainable Development Goals
- 17 SDGs
- Societal issues where Artificial Intelligence can solve the issues

Objective Bot

- Understand the social issues in the world
- Know who is a responsible citizenship
- Learn about 17 Sustainable Development Goals

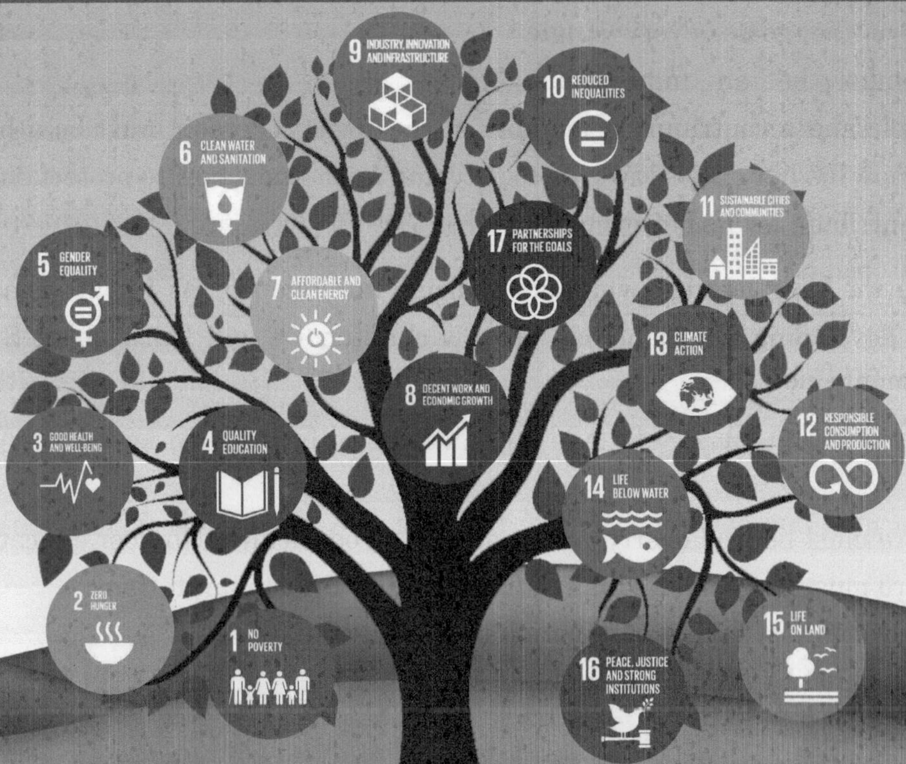

Introduction to Sustainable Development Goals

From the past 200 years, we have moved from an agricultural to an industrial and then to a digital age. In an industrial age, there has been many discovery and invention and this age defines many new social dynamics which affects in every part of human life.

For the achievement of the goals which we are imagining, we need to put our efforts and see what we can do in the next two or three years instead of focusing or planning goals for the next ten years.

To achieve the goals, every single person must be an industrious, responsible and a contributing member of the society. Person must be a helpful and should know his/her duties towards society and must know how to protect environment and to contribute for its betterment.

Till now, we have learned what is Artificial Intelligence, its applications. How AI helps in developing Smart homes. In this chapter, we will learn about Sustainable Development Goals.

Various social themes, which every citizen must known to be a responsible citizen:

- There must be No Poverty, No Hunger, No Poor health, No Poor education
- There must be Gender equality, Clean water, Proper sanitation
- Everyone must take proper action to protect climate
- There must be Peace and Justice

Fact Bot

Sustainable Development Goals are the result of a three-year process which involves eighty-three national surveys.

Activity I

Match and identify the various social themes given in Column A with Column B, which is the responsibility of every citizen to Eradicate form the society.

Column A	Column B
	Peace
	Education
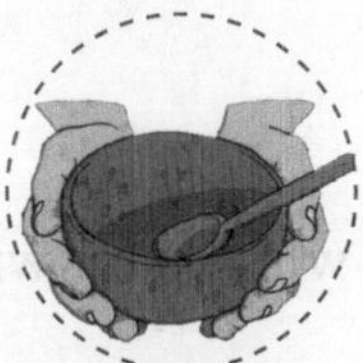	Inequality
	Cleanliness and Sanitation
	Hunger

Sustainable Development Goals

Sustainable Development Goals as per the UNESCO 2030 has seventeen Goals, which come on effect from January 1, 2016. These Goals will create many positive changes in the local communities of many countries.

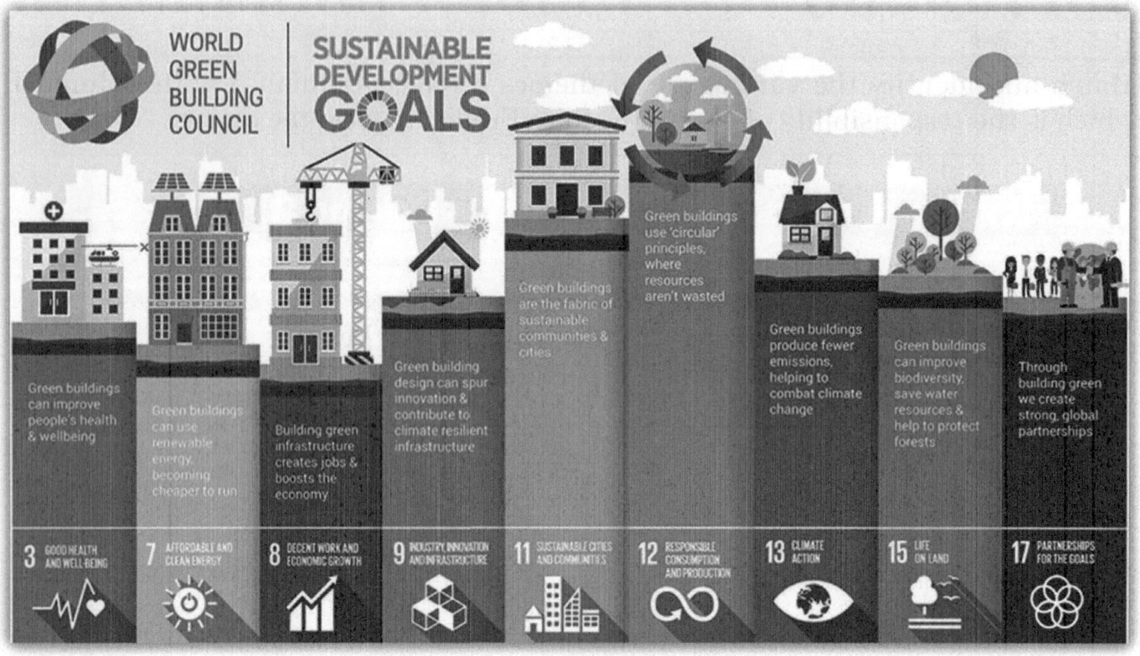

UNESCO 2030 17 SDGs

With Sustainable Development Goals, you will:

- Grow up in an interconnected and multicultural society in which you will learn about the various cultural norms.
- Be an active participant in your community and help the society to solve the world's biggest challenge.
- Know the various challenges such as sanitation, poverty, education, hunger.

DEFINITION

The Sustainable Development Goals (SDGs) are the collection of 17 Global Goals which are designed to be a blueprint in order to achieve a better and the more sustainable future for all.

Activity II

AI for Oceans

1. Visit the link: https://code.org/oceans
2. The following screen appear:

3. Click on Try now.
4. The following page appears, on the top it is highlighting 1, play the video.

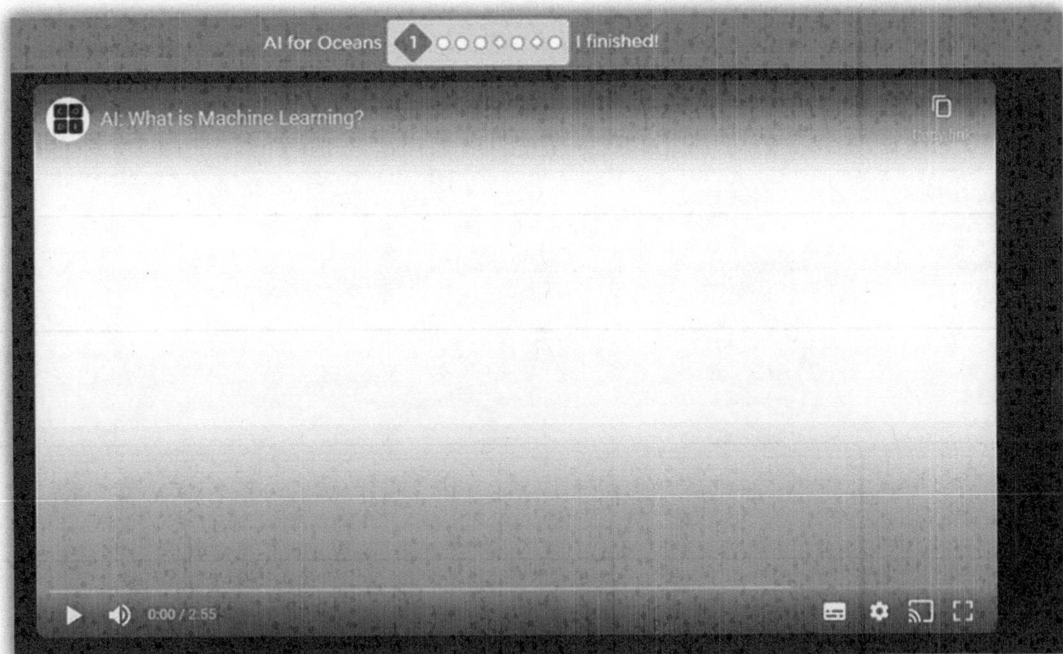

5. Video will explain about Artificial Intelligence, Machine Learning, how computer recognise data and make decision.

6. Watch the video and write your observation about how Machine learning is useful in our day to day life:

What is Sustainable Development Goal?

The Sustainable Development Goals (SDGs) are the collection of 17 Global Goals which are designed to be a blueprint in order to achieve a better and the more sustainable future for all. The SDGs, are set in 2015 by the United Nations General Assembly and is intended to be achieved by the year 2030, and is a part of UN Resolution 70/1, the 2030 Agenda.

The Sustainable Development Goals are:

Goal No	Sustainable Development Goals (SDGs)	Description
1.	**No Poverty**  End poverty in all its form from everywhere.	• Its target is to end the extreme poverty globally by 2030. • People live in poverty if they do not have the basic services such as healthcare, security, and education.
2	**Zero Hunger**  End hunger, to achieve food security to improve nutrition, and to promote sustainable agriculture.	• It states that by 2030 we should end hunger and all forms of malnutrition.
3	**Good Health and Well-being**  Healthy lives and promote well-being for all.	• It aims to increase the life expectancy and reduce common killers which are associated with child and maternal mortality.

4	**Quality Education**  Ensure inclusive and equitable quality education and promote lifelong learning opportunities for all.	• It aims to provide education, at primary school level, for both boys and girls.
5	**Gender Equality**  Achieve gender equality and to empower all women and girls.	• It's a stand-alone goal, which aims for women to receive the same attention as of men.
6	**Clean Water and Sanitation**  Ensure availability and sustainable management of water and sanitation for all.	• It has eight targets and 11 indicators which will be used to monitor the progress toward the targets, to be achieved by the year 2030 and one by 2020. • The first three targets are related to drinking water supply and sanitation.
7	**Affordable and Clean Energy**  Ensure access to affordable, sustainable, reliable and modern energy for all.	• Its targets is to provide an affordable and reliable energy.

8	**Decent Work and Economic Growth**  Promote sustained, inclusive and sustainable economic growth for all.	• Its aim is to attain at least 7 percent annual growth in gross domestic product (GDP). • The target is to reduce the youth unemployment and operationalize a global strategy.
9	**Industry, Innovation, and Infrastructure**  Build, promote resilient infrastructure, sustainable industrialization, and foster the innovation.	• It aims to provide employment to people in manufacturing industry.
10	**Reducing Inequality**  Reduce the income inequality within and among the countries.	• Its aim is to "sustain the income growth of the bottom forty percent of the population at a higher rate than the national average".

11	**Sustainable Cities and Communities**  Make the cities and the human settlements safe, sustainable, and resilient.	• Its aim is to ensure the access to safe and affordable housing to everyone.
12	**Responsible Consumption and Production**  Ensure the sustainable consumption and the production patterns.	• It aims to use eco-friendly production methods and thus reduce the amount of waste.
13	**Climate Action**  Combat the climate change and impacts by regulating emissions and also promoting developments in renewable energy.	• Its aim is to take actions against global warming.

<table>
<tr>
<td>14</td>
<td>Life Below Water

Conserve and use the seas, marines and ocean resources sustainably for sustainable development.</td>
<td>• Its aim is to create effective strategies to reduce the adverse effects of the increased ocean acidification and to protect the marine biodiversity.</td>
</tr>
<tr>
<td>15</td>
<td>Life On Land

Protect, restore and promote the sustainable use of terrestrial ecosystems, which includes managing the forests, desertification, halt and reverse the land degradation, biodiversity loss.</td>
<td>• It aims is to preserve biodiversity of desert, forest, and mountain eco-systems.</td>
</tr>
<tr>
<td>16</td>
<td>Peace, Justice, and Strong Institutions

Promote peaceful and inclusive societies for the sustainable development, by providing access to justice for all.</td>
<td>• Its aims is to reduce violent crime, sex trafficking, forced labour, child abuse and all forms of violence and torture against children.</td>
</tr>
</table>

17	**Partnerships for the Goals**  Strengthen the implementation and revitalize the global partnership for the sustainable development.	• It aim to assure that countries and the organizations cooperate and developing multi-stakeholder partnerships to share the knowledge, technology, and financial support.

Tip Bot

Water Conservation is a global issue.

Activity III

Identify and write the Name of Sustainable Development Goal.

Memory Bot

Idea of Sustainable Development Goals came from the Rio+20 Summit in 2012, which is the largest summit in the UN history.

Check your Progress - I

State whether the following statements are True or False.

a The Sustainable Development Goals (SDGs) are the collection of 17 Global Goals. True/False

b SDGs are designed to be a blueprint to achieve a better and the more sustainable future for all. True/False

c The SDGs, are set in 1990 by the United Nations General Assembly. True/False

Answer: True, True, False.

Goals

The SDGs are broad based and are interdependent. The 17 Sustainable Development Goals have a list of targets which are to be measured with the indicators.

To make the SDGs successful, all the data on the 17 Goals are available in an easy to understandable form and variety of tools are there to track and visualize the progress towards the Goals.

UNESCO's Sustainable Development Goals take initiatives to handle some of the world's greatest problems like hunger, pollution, and many socio-economic challenges. In the field of agriculture, many new AI advancements are introduced. Crop and soil monitoring uses many new algorithms and the data collected on the field is used to manage and track the health of the crops; thus making it easier and sustainable for the farmers.

Fact Bot

Solutions to Global Goals which include UNESCOs SDG Agenda 2030 requires effective planning.

Tip Bot

Goals of a social problem are identified by the data points which are collected on the basis of different sources.

Bio-medical systems which includes medical image processing, heart-sound analysis are the fundamental driving forces of the Al revolution.

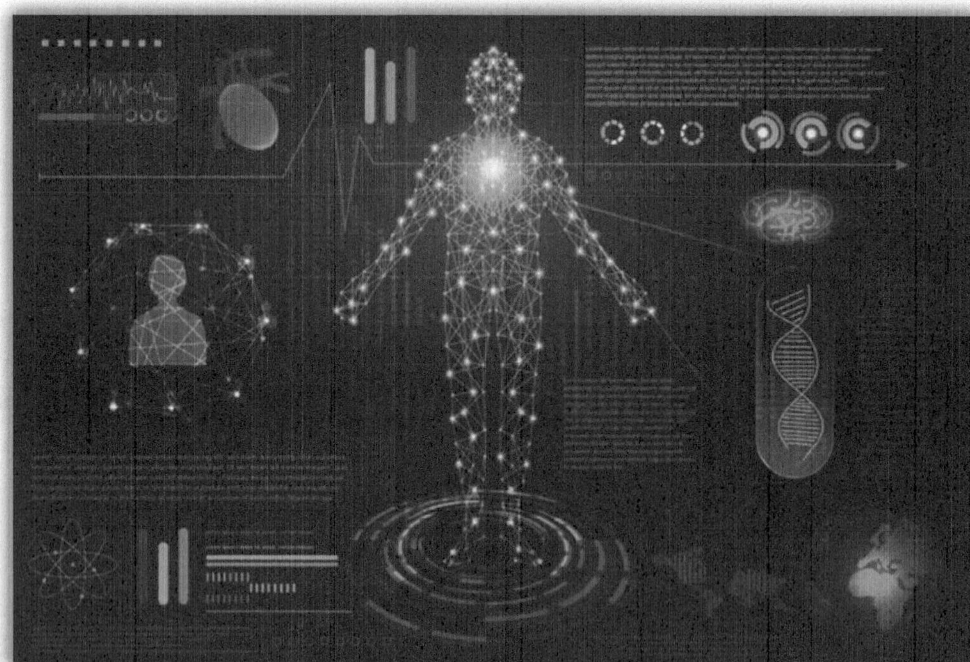

Memory Bot

Some SDGs are able to harness the data-driven approach with its advanced technologies in order to accelerate the innovation at a global scale.

Activity IV

Train Machine learning model

Description

- In this activity, you will program or train artificial intelligence model to identify whether the item coming up on the screen is fish or trash.

To play the game:

1. Visit the link: https://studio.code.org/s/oceans/stage/1/puzzle/2
2. The following screen appears:

3. Now, we are at the level 2 of the activity. We have completed the level 1 in Activity II.
4. Click anywhere on the screen to start the game, and train the AI model to clean the ocean.
5. Now the screen appears, which shows the object, you have to identify whether it is a fish or not.

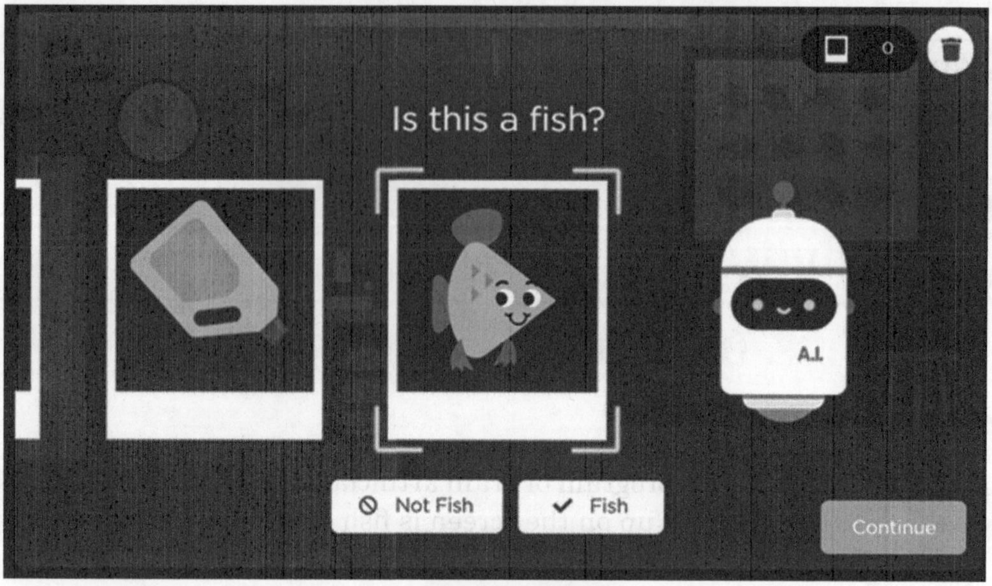

If it is fish you have to click on 

, and if the object is not fish then click on 

.

6. Continue to train the model, and once you done click on Continue.
7. Click on Run to see if A.I. knows how a "fish" looks.

8. Now, based on your training A.I. will identify the fish or trash.

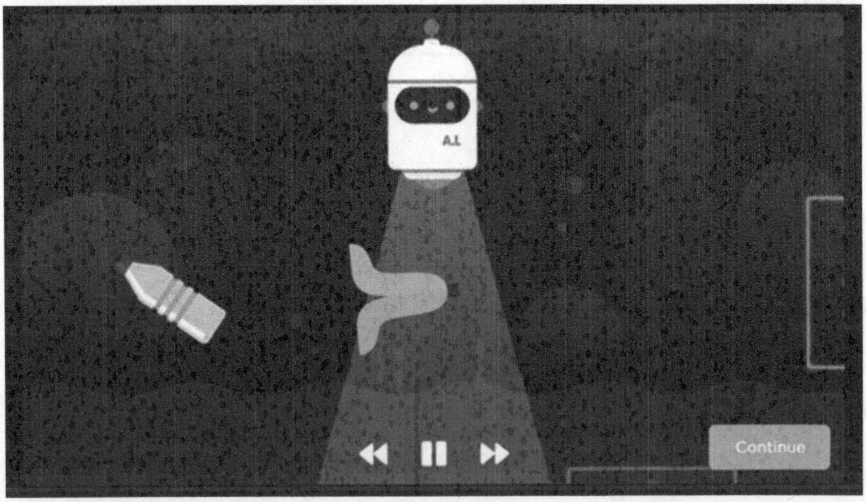

Check your Progress - II

Fill in the Blanks.

Hint: 70/1, Sustainable Development Goals, 2015

a. The ________ are the collection of 17 Global Goals.

b. The SDGs, are set in ________ by the United Nations General Assembly.

c. SDGs are a part of UN Resolution________, the 2030 Agenda.

Answer: Sustainable, 2015, 70/1, Development Goals

Role of Artificial Intelligence in Sustainable Development

Artificial Intelligence helps us to solve the complex and interrelated global challenges which include hunger, change in climate and life on land. AI processes are used to computerize the routine tasks, analyse the big data, generating the solutions to many sustainable development issues. If an AI solution is designed in a well manner than it can play a transformative role in achieving, the SDGs.

AI gives an extraordinary result with the correct vision in mind and its purpose is to bring good to humanity.

Definition

Zero hunger means to "*End hunger, achieve the food security, to improved nutrition, and to promote sustainable agriculture*".

Activity V

Understand the problem, concern and research

Description

Consider Goal 13 of Sustainable Development Goal: Climate Action

Observation

- Change in climate is increasing day by day
- Impact on the climate can be seen and is impacting everyone's life

Result of the activity:

- We will able to scope the problem of the climate change.
- Know about the hierarchy of the problem and get to know how the problems can be solved.

Click on the link:

https://www.youtube.com/watch?v=IJoAcD0oUww; watch the video and write your observation of change in climate:

- ____
  ____
- ____
  ____
- ____
  ____
- ____
  ____
- ____
  ____

Fact Bot

In some of the workable Goals like No Hunger; Good Health & well-being; Life on Land; Artificial intelligence has played a constructive role in giving solutions for the challenges faced.

Activity VI

Train AI to detect whether the object belongs to water or not

In activity IV, we have trained AI model to detect if the object is fish or not, now in this activity we will train the AI model to detect whether the object belongs to water or not.

1. Go to the following link https://studio.code.org/s/oceans/stage/1/puzzle/4.
2. The following screen appears:

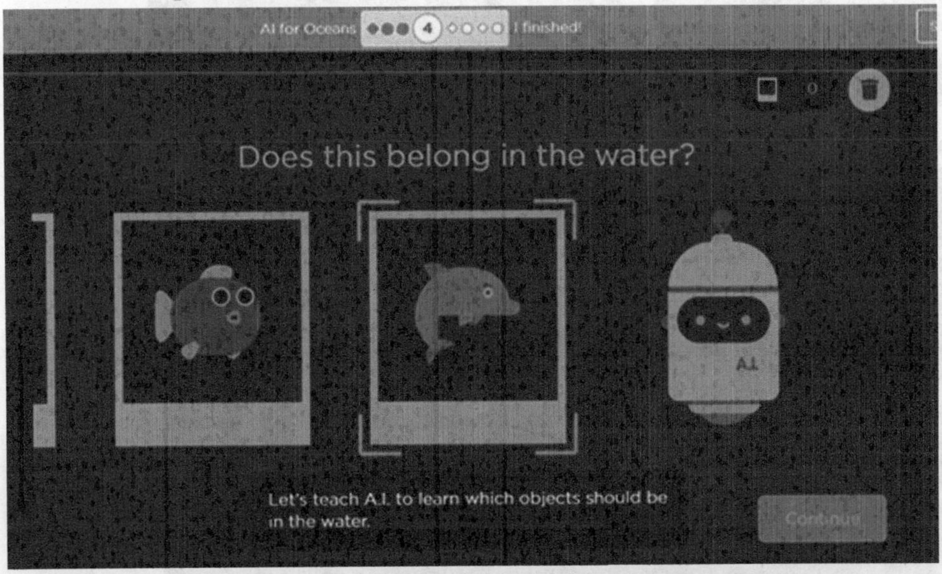

3. In this you will teach A.I. to learn whether the object belongs to water or not.
4. If the object belongs to water click 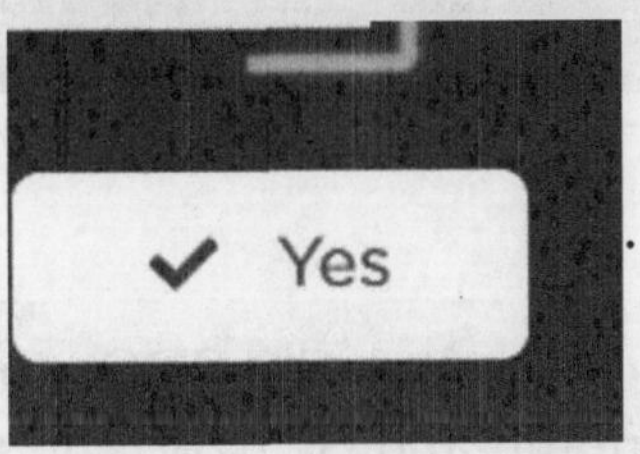

.

And if it does not belongs to water click  .

5. Click Continue, now A.I. model will detect the object as per your training.

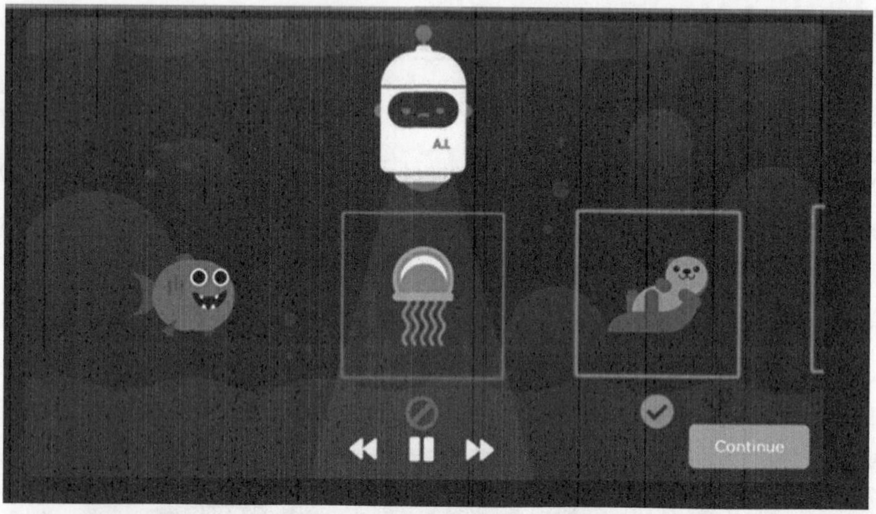

6. On the basis of training, here are some object which are identified by A.I.

Tip Bot

Country most likely to complete the SDGs first is Sweden, according to one report. Norway, Denmark, Finland and Switzerland are close behind.

Check your Progress - III

Tick the correct option.

a Artificial Intelligence helps us to solve **complex/simple** and interrelated global challenges which include hunger, change in climate and life on land.

b AI processes are used to computerize the **routine tasks/ non routine task**, analyse the big data, generating the solutions to many sustainable development issues.

c AI gives an **extraordinary/ordinary** result with the correct vision in mind and its purpose is to bring good to humanity.

Answer: complex, routine task, extraordinary

Memory Bot

The 35-page United Nations text outlining the post-2015 development agenda which is: "*A plan of action for people, planet and prosperity*,"

TECH BOT

- **Sustainable Development Goals (SDGs):** Collection of 17 Global Goals which are designed to be a blueprint in order to achieve a better and the more sustainable future for all.
- **No Poverty:** End poverty in all its form from everywhere.
- **Zero Hunger:** End hunger, to achieve food security to improved nutrition, and to promote sustainable agriculture

Recap Bot

- From the past 200 years, we have moved from an agricultural to an industrial and then to a digital age.
- In an industrial age, there has been many discovery and invention and this age defines many new social dynamics which affects in every part of human life.
- To achieve the Goals, every single person must be an industrious, responsible and a contributing member of the society.

- Various social themes, which every citizen must known to be a responsible citizen:
  - There must be No Poverty, No Hunger, No Poor health, No Poor education
  - There must be Gender equality, Clean water, Proper sanitation
  - Everyone must take proper action to protect climate
  - There must be Peace and Justice
- Sustainable Development Goals as per the United Nations has seventeen Sustainable Development Goals (SDGs), which come on effect from January 1, 2016. These Goals will create many positive changes in the local communities of many countries.
- The Sustainable Development Goals (SDGs) are the collection of 17 Global Goals which are designed to be a blueprint in order to achieve a better and the more sustainable future for all.
- The SDGs, are set in 2015 by the United Nations General Assembly and is intended to be achieved by the year 2030, and is a part of UN Resolution 70/1, the 2030 Agenda.
- The Sustainable Development Goals are:
  - **No Poverty:** End poverty in all its form from everywhere.
  - **Zero Hunger:** End hunger, to achieve food security to improved nutrition, and to promote sustainable agriculture.
  - **Good Health and Well-being:** Healthy lives and promote well-being for all.
  - **Quality Education:** Ensure inclusive and equitable quality education and promote lifelong learning opportunities for all.
  - **Gender Equality:** Achieve gender equality and to empower all women and girls.
  - **Clean Water and Sanitation:** Ensure availability and sustainable management of water and sanitation for all.
  - **Affordable and Clean Energy:** Ensure access to affordable, sustainable, reliable and modern energy for all.
  - **Decent Work and Economic Growth:** Promote sustained, inclusive and sustainable economic growth for all.
  - **Industry, Innovation, and Infrastructure:** Build, promote resilient infrastructure, sustainable industrialization, and foster the innovation.
  - **Reducing Inequality:** Reduce the income inequality within and among the countries.

- **Sustainable Cities and Communities:** Make the cities and the human settlements safe, sustainable, and resilient.
- **Responsible Consumption and Production:** Ensure the sustainable consumption and the production patterns
- **Climate Action:** Combat the climate change and impacts by regulating emissions and also promoting developments in renewable energy.
- **Life below Water:** Conserve and use the seas, marines and ocean resources sustainably for sustainable development.
- **Life on Land:** Protect, restore and promote the sustainable use of terrestrial ecosystems, which includes managing the forests, desertification, halt and reverse the land degradation, biodiversity loss.
- **Peace, Justice, and Strong Institutions:** Promote peaceful and inclusive societies for the sustainable development, by providing access to justice for all.
- **Partnerships for the Goals:** Strengthen the implementation and revitalize the global partnership for the sustainable development

◆ The SDGs are broad based and are interdependent. These 17 Sustainable Development Goals have a list of targets which are to be measured with the indicators.

◆ UNESCO's Sustainable Development Goals take initiatives to handle some of the world's greatest problems like hunger, pollution, and many socio-economic challenges.

◆ Bio-medical systems which include medical image processing, heart-sound analysis are the fundamental driving forces of the Al revolution.

◆ Artificial Intelligence helps us to solve complex and interrelated global challenges which include hunger, change in climate and life on land.

◆ AI gives an extraordinary result with the correct vision in mind and its purpose is to bring good to humanity.

Brain Bot

A. MULTIPLE CHOICE QUESTIONS.

1. SDG is:
   a. Sustainable Development Goals ☐
   b. Sustain Development Goals ☐
   c. Single Development Goals ☐
   d. Sustainable Design Goals ☐
2. How many SDGs are there?
   a. 15 ☐ b. 16 ☐
   c. 17 ☐ d. 18 ☐
3. Agenda of Sustainable Development Goals is aim to be achieved by:
   a. 2010 ☐ b. 2020 ☐
   c. 2030 ☐ d. 2030 ☐
4. Seventeen Sustainable Development Goals fall under the _____ three domain pillars.
   a. 3 ☐ b. 4 ☐
   c. 5 ☐ d. 6 ☐
5. Aim of Goal 13 is to take actions against:
   a. Poverty ☐ b. Global warming ☐
   c. Hunger ☐ d. Gender equality ☐

B. FILL IN THE BLANKS.

Hints: January 1, poverty, hunger, increase, education

1. Sustainable Development Goals come on effect form __________, 2016.
2. Target of Goal 1 is to end the extreme __________ globally.
3. Goal 2 states that by 2030 we should end __________.
4. Goal 3 aims to __________ life expectancy.
5. Goal 4 aims to provide __________.

C. MATCH THE FOLLOWING.

	Column A		Column B
1.	Affordable and Clean Energy	i.	
2.	Decent Work and Economic Growth	ii.	
3.	Industry, Innovation, and Infrastructure	iii.	
4.	Reducing Inequality	iv.	
5.	Sustainable Cities and Communities	v.	

D. ANSWER THE FOLLOWING QUESTIONS.

1. Define the term Sustainable Development Goals.

2. Write the name of the Goal 5.

3. What is the aim of Goal 12?

4. Briefly explain the meaning of Goal 1?

5. Write any two ways of how to achieve Gender equality.

Lab Activity Sustainable Development Goals

1. Visit the link: https://spark.adobe.com/page/rxiklnYrUvB9t/.
2. Scroll down the page and play the video:

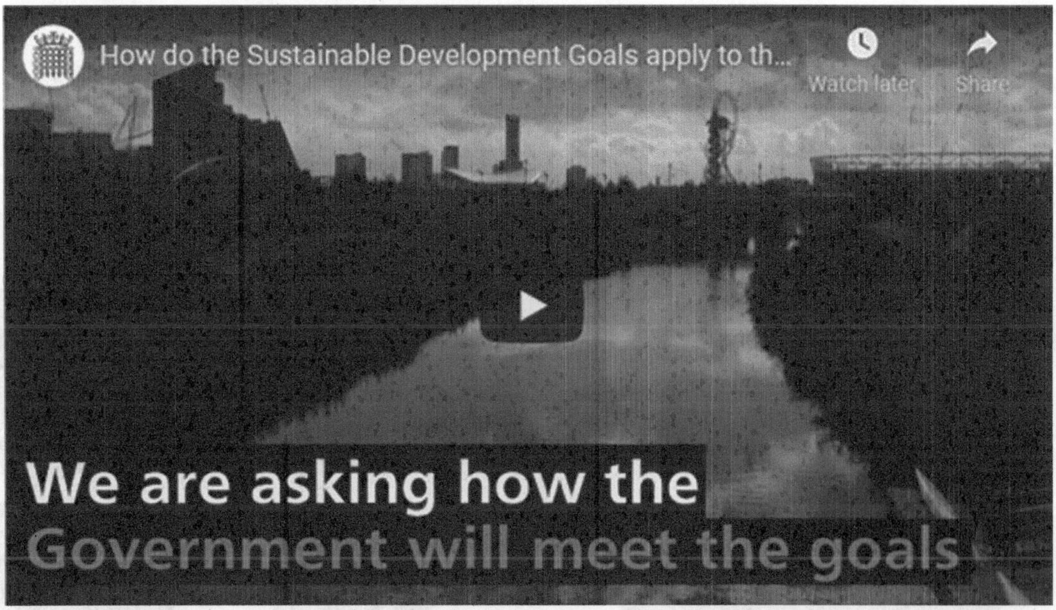

3. Scroll down the page, and read what steps government is taking to attain the Sustainable Development:

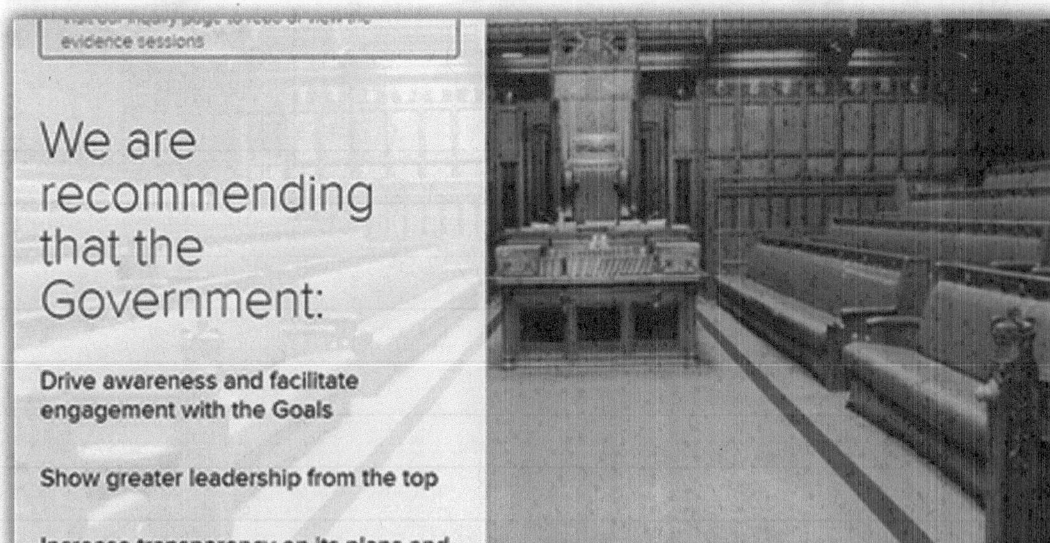

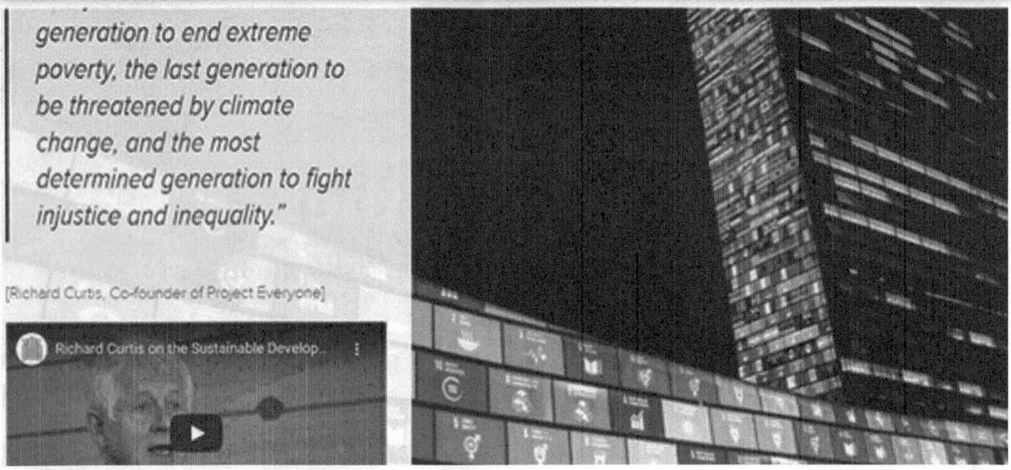

4. Write your observation:

WORKSHEET

A. STATE WHETHER THE FOLLOWING STATEMENT ARE TRUE OR FALSE.

1. To achieve the Goals, every single person must be an industrious, responsible and a contributing member of the society. True/False
2. Person must be a helpful and should know his/her duties towards society and must know how to protect environment and to contribute for its betterment. True/False
3. Sustainable Development Goals are the result of a one-year process which involves eighty-three national surveys. True/False
4. Sustainable Development Goals as per the United Nations has Twenty Sustainable Development Goals (SDGs), which come on effect from January 1, 2016. True/False
5. Sustainable Development Goals will create many positive changes in the local communities of many countries. True/False

B. FILL IN THE BLANKS.

Hints: 70/1, multicultural, 17, Healthy lives, 2015

1. With Sustainable Development Goals, you will grow up in an interconnected and ___________ society in which you will learn about the various cultural norms.
2. The Sustainable Development Goals (SDGs) are the collection of ___________ Global Goals.
3. The SDGs, are set in ___________ by the United Nations General Assembly.
4. SDGs is intended to be achieved by the year 2030, and is a part of UN Resolution___________, the 2030 Agenda.
5. Good Health and Well-being means to have ___________ and promote well-being for all.

C. ANSWER THE FOLLOWING QUESTIONS.

1. Name various social themes, which every citizen must known to become a responsible citizen.

2. What is the main goal of inklewriter?

3. Write the name of the Goal 8 of SDGs.

4. What is the aim of Goal 15 of SDGs?

5. Briefly explain the meaning of Goal 17 of SDGs

Quiz Card

TICK THE CORRECT ANSWER.

1. Sustainable Development focuses on
   - a economic development
   - b social development
   - c environmental protection
   - d all of the above
2. As per United Nations, _______ is the issue(s) of human development.
   - a education
   - b public health
   - c poverty
   - d all of the above
3. United Nations (UN) decade of education for sustainable development is from
   - a 2002-10
   - b 2003-11
   - c 2004-13
   - d 2005-14
4. Numbers of Sustainable Development Goals (SDGs) by United Nations are
   - a 14
   - b 15
   - c 16
   - d 17
5. Sustainable development will design a systems which is
   - a flexible and irreversible
   - b flexible and reversible
   - c inflexible and reversible
   - d inflexible and irreversible
6. Element(s) of sustainable agriculture are:
   - a permaculture
   - b agroforestry
   - c mixed farming
   - d all of the above
7. Sustainable energy is
   - a clean
   - b used over a long period of time
   - c both (a) and (b)
   - d none of the above
8. The criterion for corporate sustainability is
   - a eco-efficiency
   - b socio-efficiency
   - c both (a) and (b)
   - d none of the above
9. Four domains of circles of sustainability, used by the United Nations are:
   - a economic, ecological, political and cultural
   - b economic, social, political and cultural
   - c economic, ecological, social and cultural
   - d economic, ecological, political and social
10. The United Nations Conference on Sustainable Development (UNCSD) is also known as
    - a Rio 2010
    - b Rio 2011
    - c Rio 2012
    - d Rio 2013

Notes

PROJECT

Get ready for SMART CITY

Smarter Home

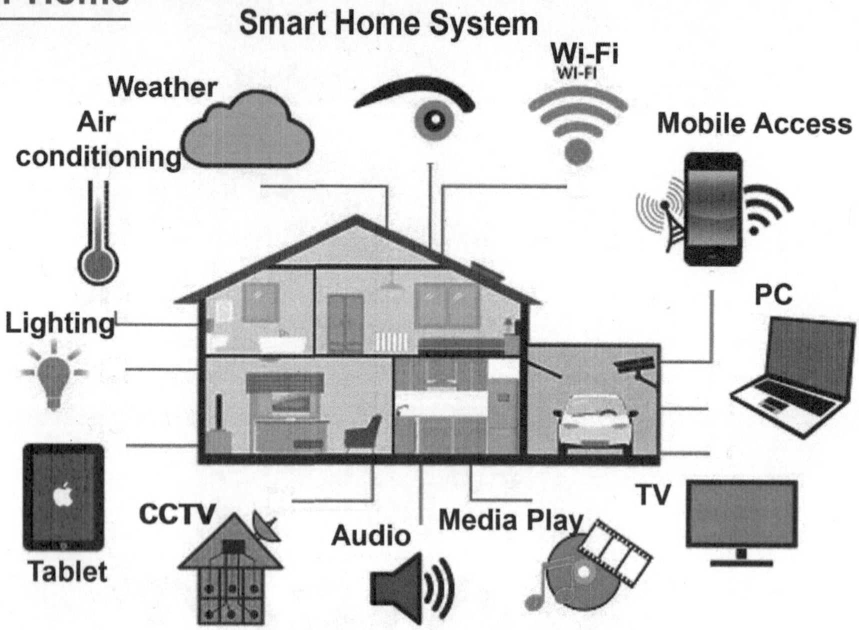

Smarter Hospital

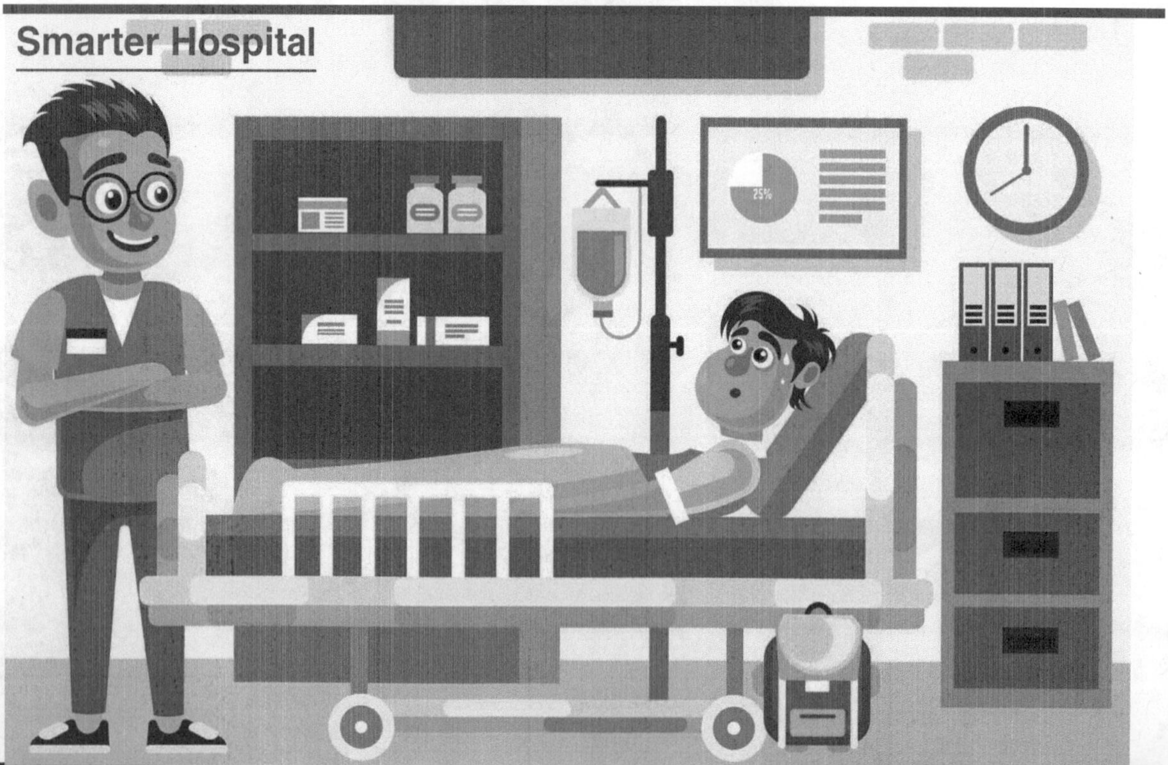

DESIGNING A HOME USING LUCIDCHART

Lucidchart helps the users to sketch and share the professional flowchart diagrams, providing designs for anything from brainstorming to project management.

Lucidchart helps you to visually solve the complex problems by creating architectural diagrams and flow charts which create clarity. It allows multiple team members to collaborate at the same time, thus making it easy to work across a fully distributed team."

To start with Lucid chart:

1. Visit the link: https://www.lucidchart.com/pages/
2. Sign up for the account.
3. The following screen appears:

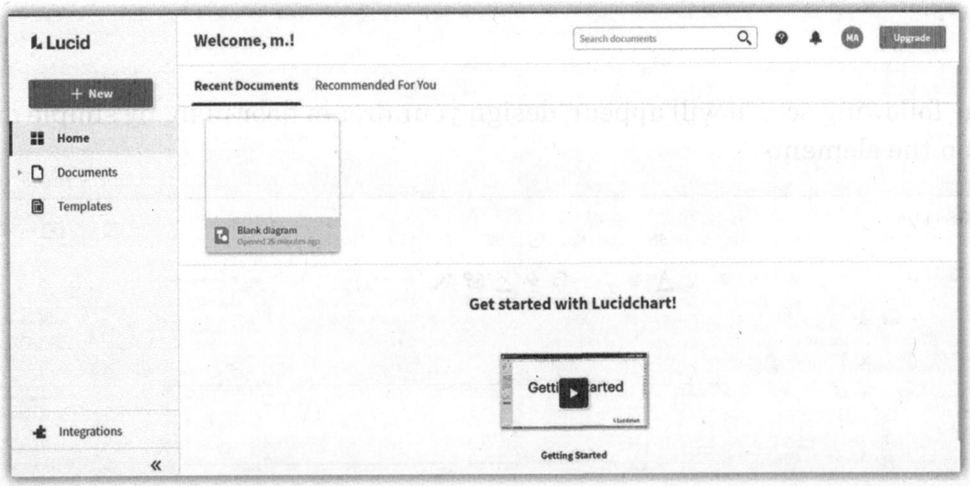

4. Click on New and select start with a template.
5. The following screen appears:

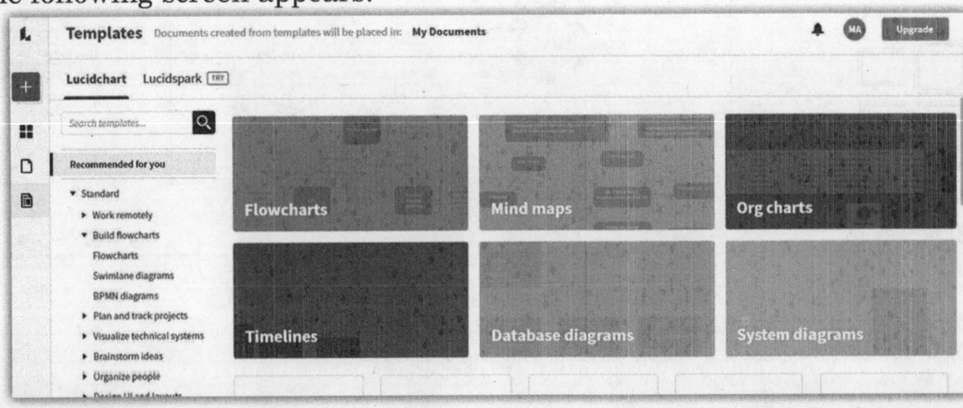

6. Type floor plan in the search box and the following options will appear, choose any one from the given options and then click on open template.

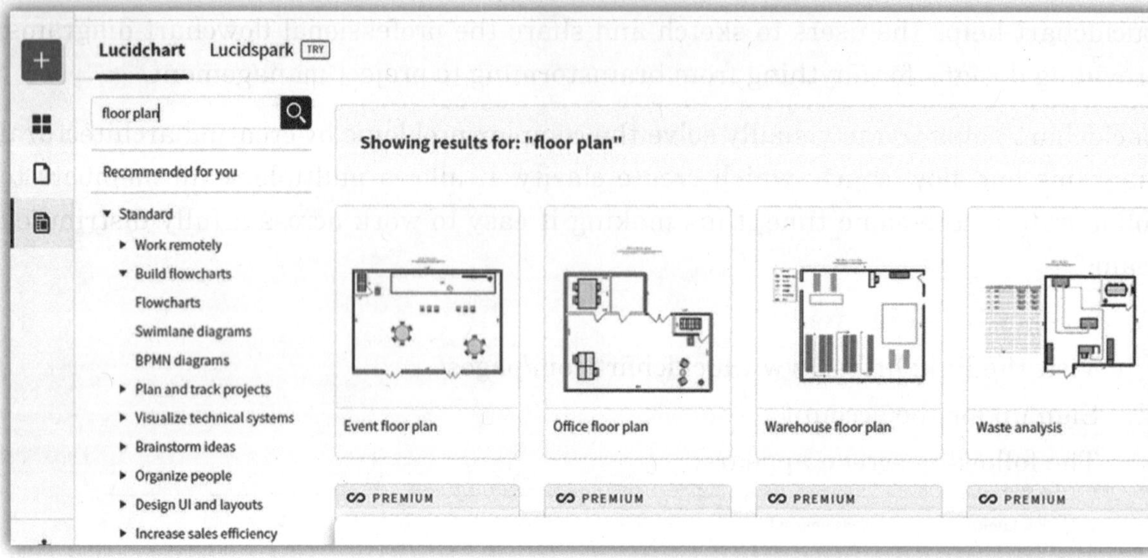

7. The following screen will appear, design your dream floor plan, by simple drag and drop the elements.

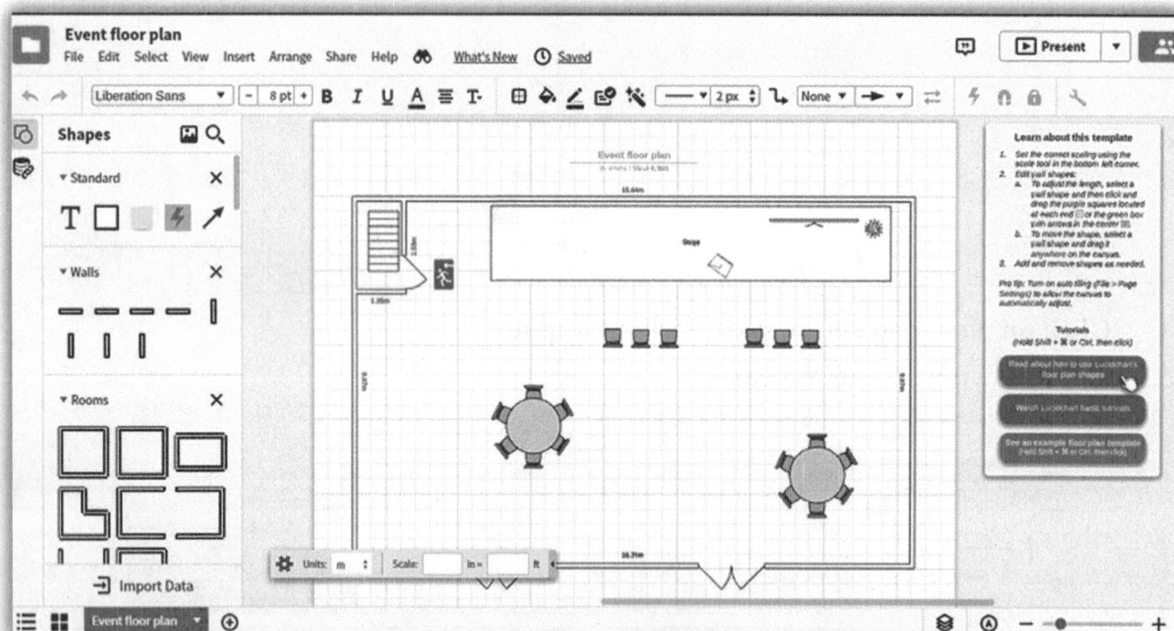

Example of floor plan:

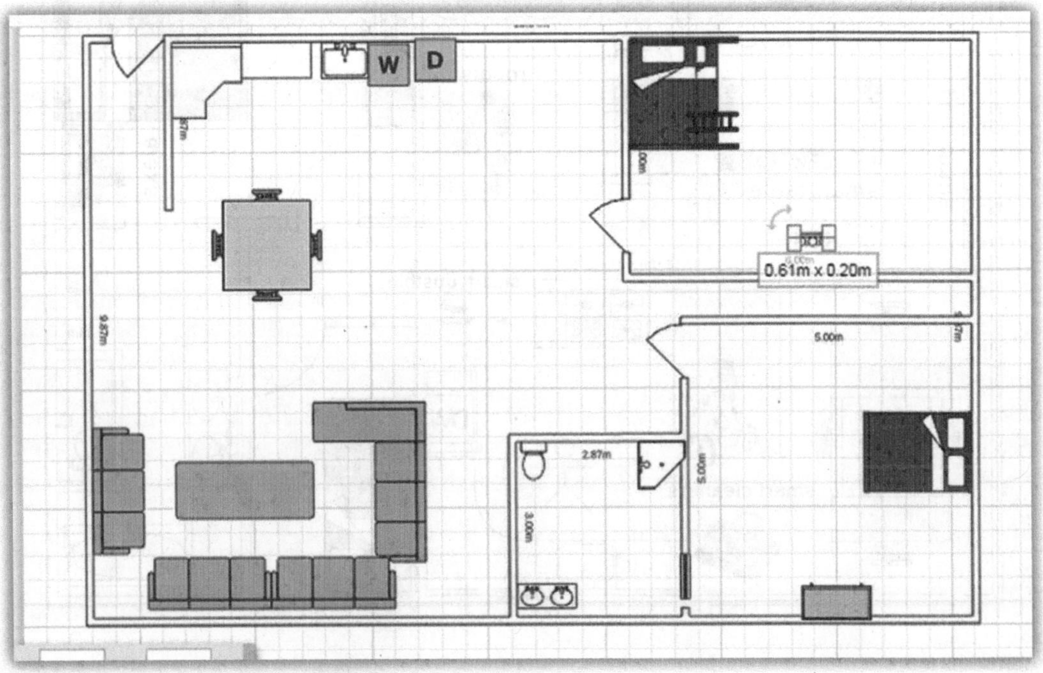

Example of Smart Home Plan:

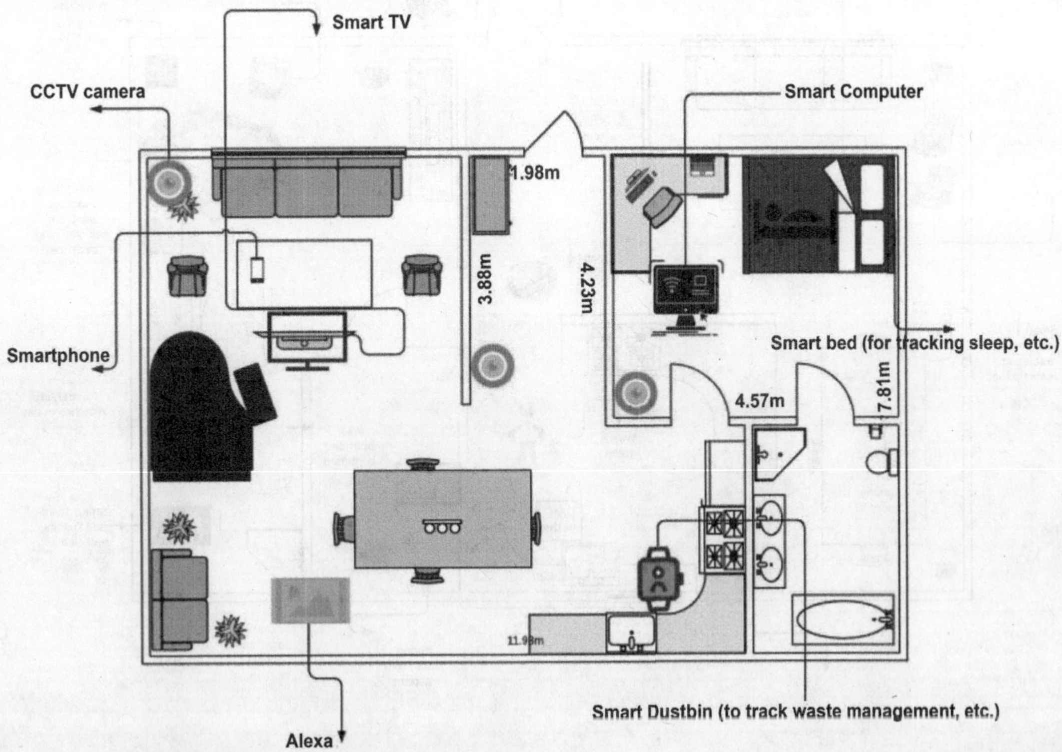

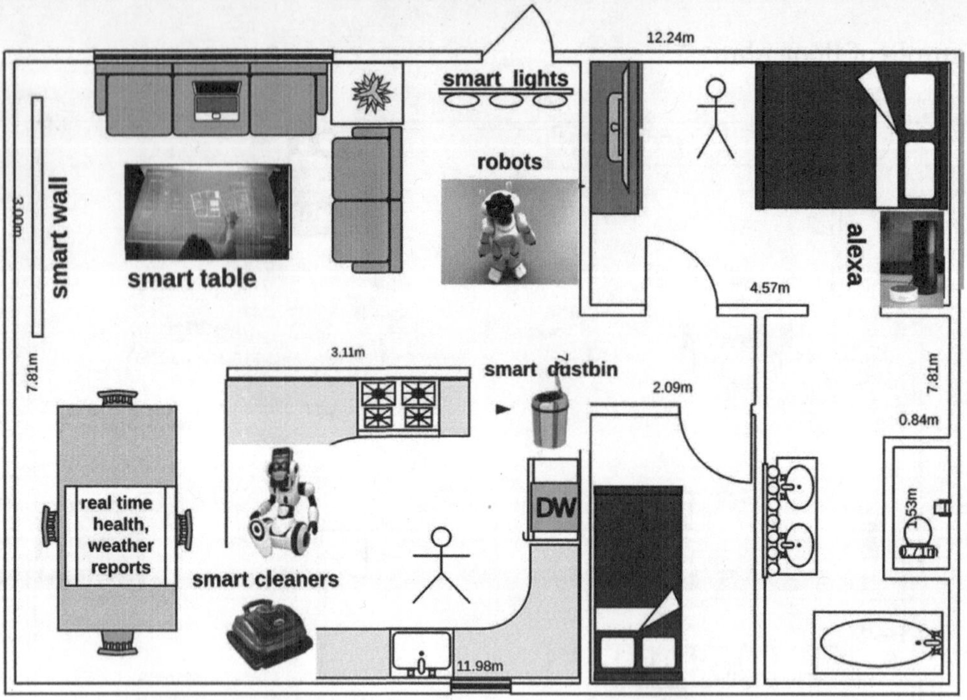
12.24m
smart lights
robots
smart wall
3.00m
smart table
alexa
4.57m
3.11m
smart dustbin
2.09m
7.81m
7.81m
0.84m
real time health, weather reports
DW
smart cleaners
11.98m

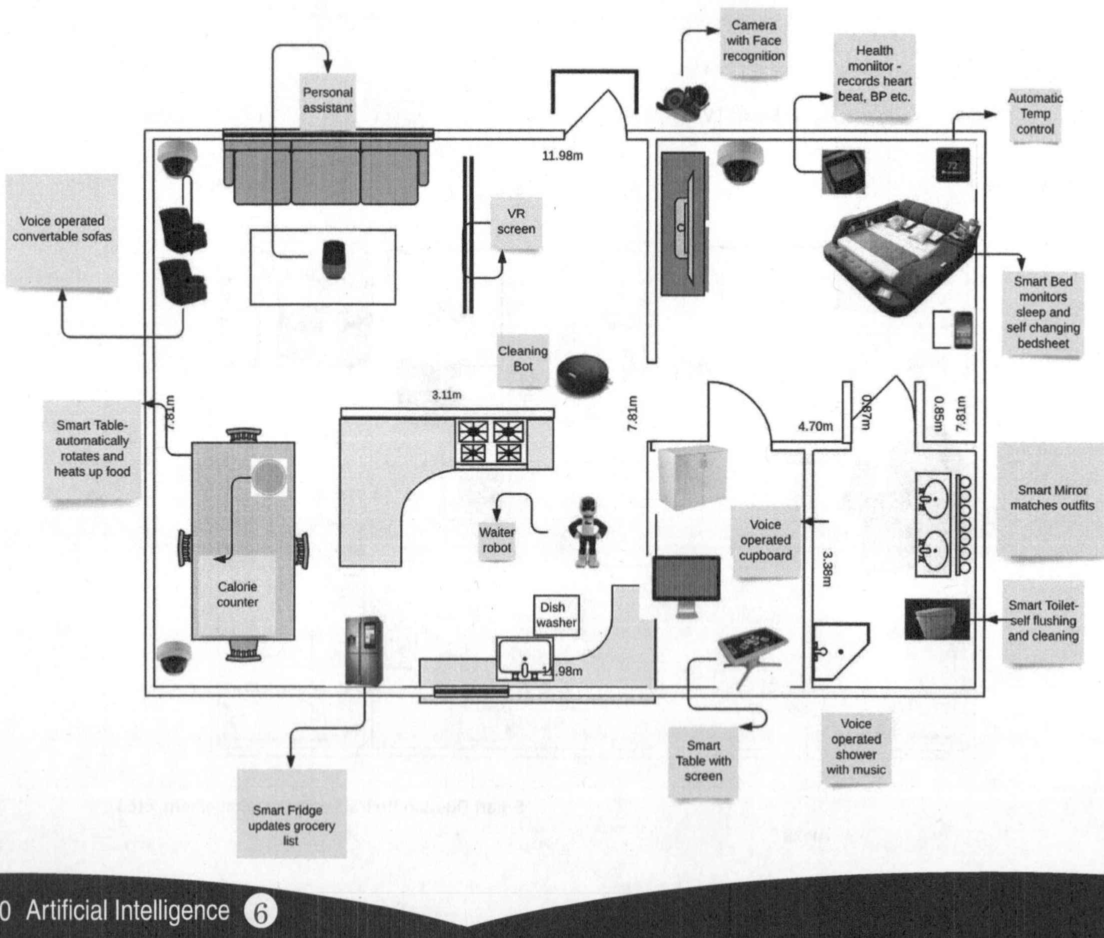
Personal assistant
Camera with Face recognition
Health moniitor - records heart beat, BP etc.
Automatic Temp control
11.98m
Voice operated convertable sofas
VR screen
Smart Bed monitors sleep and self changing bedsheet
Cleaning Bot
3.11m
7.81m
4.70m
0.87m
0.85m
7.81m
7.81m
Smart Table- automatically rotates and heats up food
Smart Mirror matches outfits
Waiter robot
Voice operated cupboard
3.38m
Calorie counter
Dish washer
11.98m
Smart Toilet- self flushing and cleaning
Smart Table with screen
Voice operated shower with music
Smart Fridge updates grocery list

Automatic Door Unlocking System Using Face Recognition in PictoBlox

PictoBlox

- PictoBlox is a Scratch 3.0-based graphical programming software.
- It is an ideal companion for the setting the first step into the world of programming.
- Its user-friendly interface and drag-and-drop functionality eliminate the need to memorize syntax and rules.
- In this we only require to focus on the problem at hand and develop skills such as logical reasoning and problem-solving.

To download PictoBlox

1. Visit the link: https://thestempedia.com/product/pictoblox/
2. Click on Download 
.
3. The following screen appears:

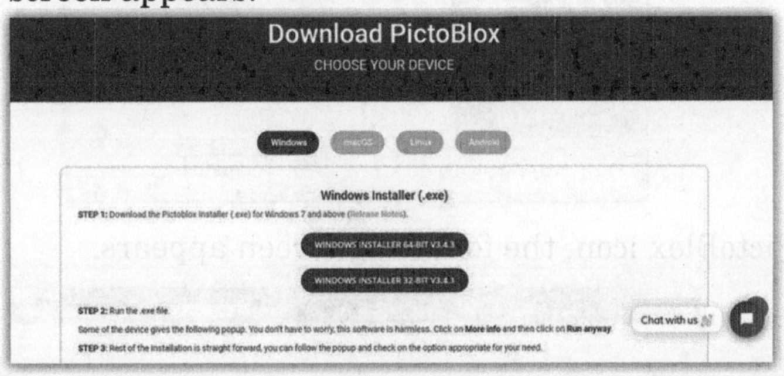

4. Choose your operating system. In this we have chosen Windows; and click on the WINDOWS INSTALLER 64-BITV3.4.3.
5. The next screen appears, ask you to enter your name and e-mail address, you can enter the required information and click on next. Or you can choose the option as No, thanks; i just want to download the PictoBlox.
6. After this the software starts downloading.
7. Once it get downloaded, click on setup file to run the exe file.

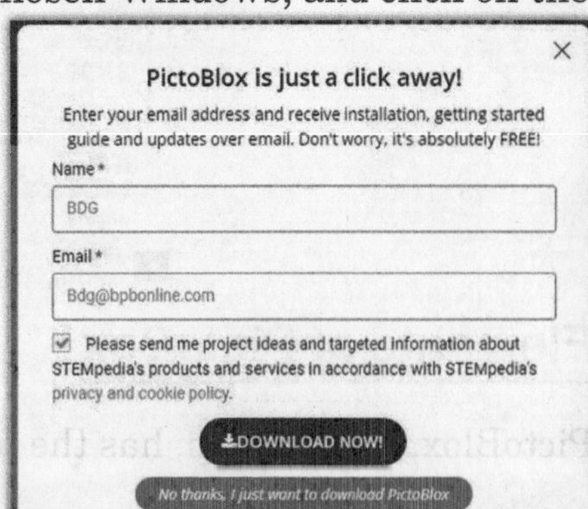

8. It will start installing the software, and ask you for the location to save the file.
9. Click on install.

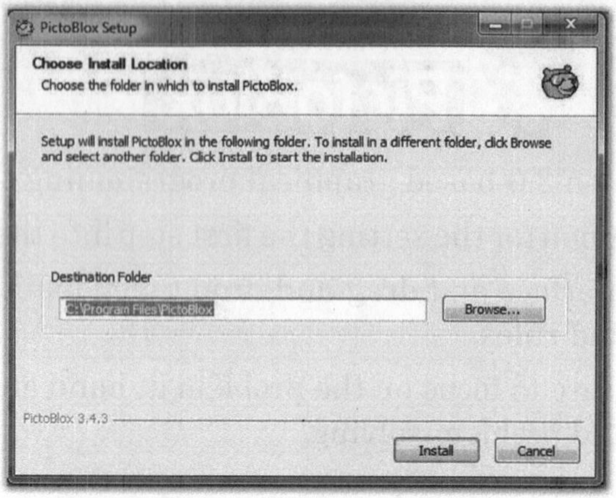

10. Once the installation gets complete, click on finish.

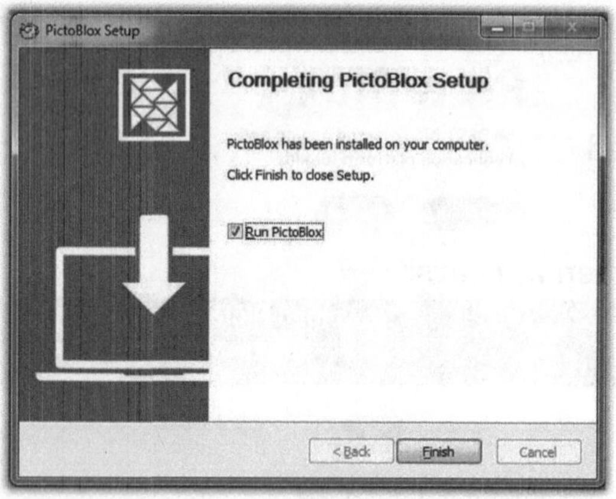

11. Click on the PictoBlox icon, the following screen appears:

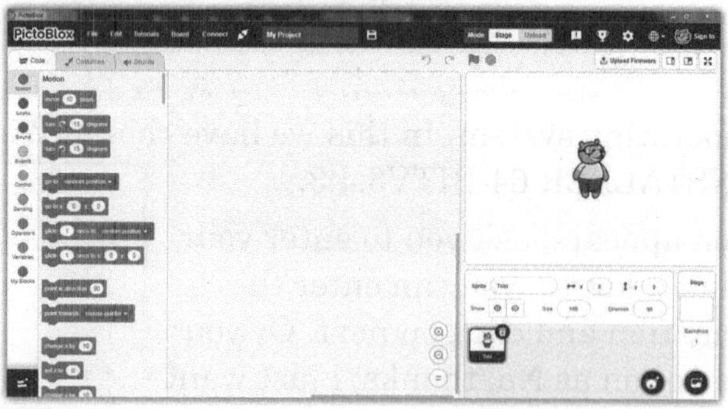

Elements of PictoBox

PictoBlox, like Scratch, has the following basic elements:

- **Sprites:** A sprite is an object, or a character, which performs different actions in the projects.
- **Stage:** The stage is the area where the sprite performs actions according to your program.
- **Script:** A script is a program or a code in PictoBlox/Scratch lingo. It is a set of 'blocks' that are arranged below one another in a specific order to perform a task or a series of tasks.
- **Blocks:** A block is like a jigsaw puzzle piece that is used to write programs by simply dragging and dropping them below one another in the scripting area.
- **Block Palette:** The block palette is under the Code tab. It consists of different palettes such as Motion, Sound, and Control.

Modes

PictoBlox has two modes:

1. **Stage Mode:** In this mode, you can write scripts for the sprite and boards like evive to interact with sprites in real-time. If you disconnect the board with Pictoblox, you cannot interact anymore.
2. **Upload Mode:** This mode allows you to write scripts and upload it to the board so that you can use even when it is not connected to your computer, for example, you need to upload a script for making moving robots.

Lets start making the Automatic Door Unlocking System Using Face Recognition

In this we will make a touch-free security system based on the face recognition technology which unlocks a door if it matches your face with the images of face you have already fed into the system.

Step 1: Prerequisites

You need to have:

a. A laptop or a computer with a camera.

b. The latest version of PictoBlox.

c. A good Internet connection.

Step 2: Setting Up the Project

a. Open PictoBlox. (Download it from: https://thestempedia.com/product/pictoblox/).

b. Click on the Add Extension button .

c. Choose Face Detection extension.

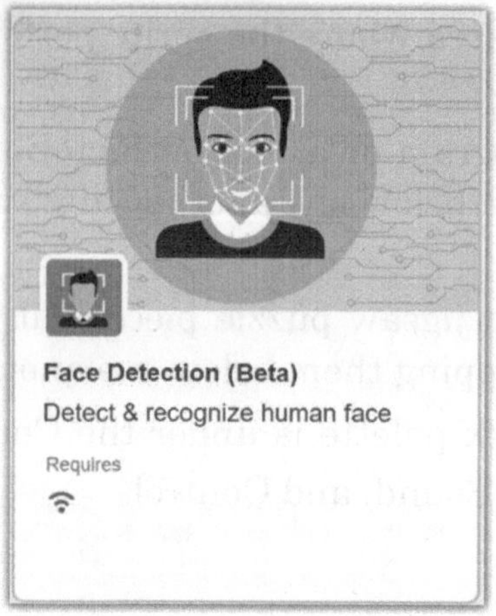

d. Also, we will use Tobi as our assistant, and make him speak.

e. Add the text-to-speech extension to make Tobi talk.

Step 3: Setting Up the Stage for Automatic Door Unlocking System

a Add the main element of the project, the door.

b Download the door. (14-15)

c Choose a Backdrop button and click on Upload Backdrop .

d Upload all the images of the door as it gives us the visual that the door is opening or closing.

e Now that we have all the door images uploaded to the project. You can remove the plain backdrop.

f Now, move Tobi to the bottom left corner.

g Let's add a small button using the ball.

h Choose a Sprite button 

i Choose the ball sprite from the library.

j The final set up will look like this.

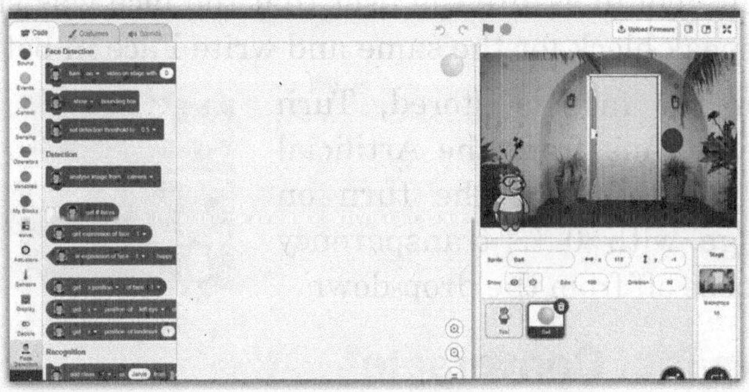

Step 4: Storing the Face into the System

a Click on Tobi's sprite.

b Place when space key pressed block from the Events palette.

c Choose space from the drop-down 

.

d Instruct Tobi to instruct the user to look into the camera.

e Place a say block from the Looks palette, and write on it "Please look into the camera".

f To make Tobi to say it loudly, place speak block from the text-to-speech palette and write the same in it.

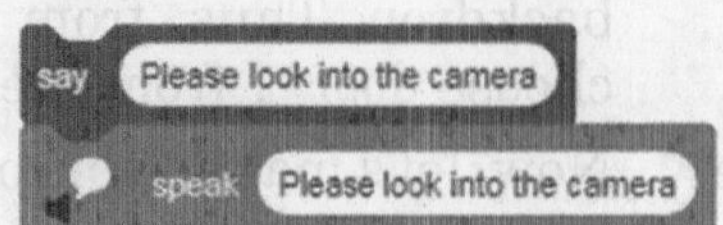

g Turn on the cameras, From the Artificial Intelligence palette, and place the turn on video on stage with 0 % transparency block.

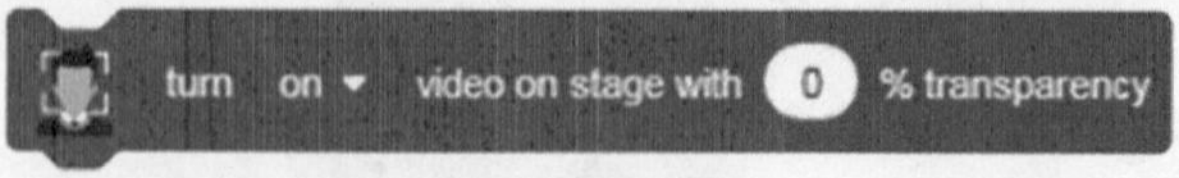

h We need the camera to analyze.

i Add wait block from the Controls palette and write 3 in the space given.

j Let's ask the user to wait for a little while.

k Add the pair of say and speak block and write Analysing in both the spaces given.

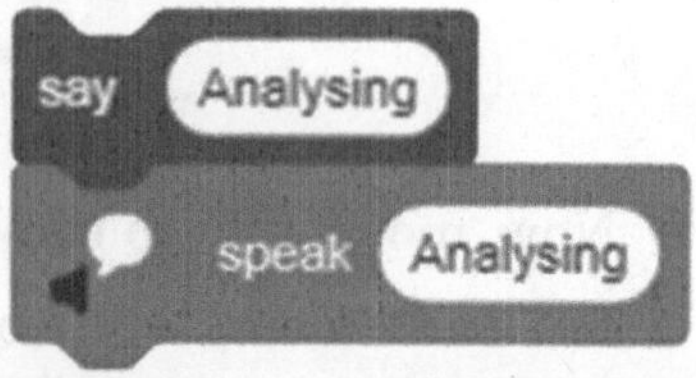

l Add the user image as the class.

m Place add class 1 as from camera.

n Write the user name into the space given.

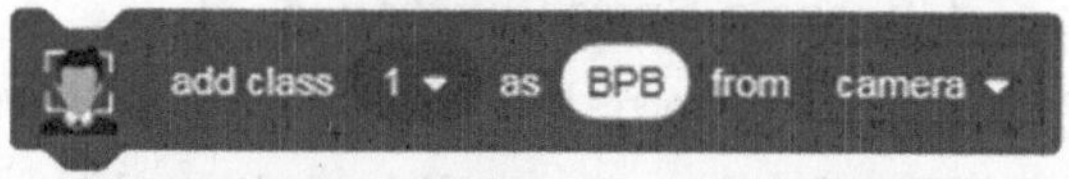

o Next, we want Tobi to assure the user that the face was stored. Thus, again use the say and speak block for the same and write Face in both the space given.

p Finally, after the face is stored, Turn off the camera, thus from the Artificial Intelligence palette, place the turn on video on stage with 0 % transparency block and choose off from the drop-down.

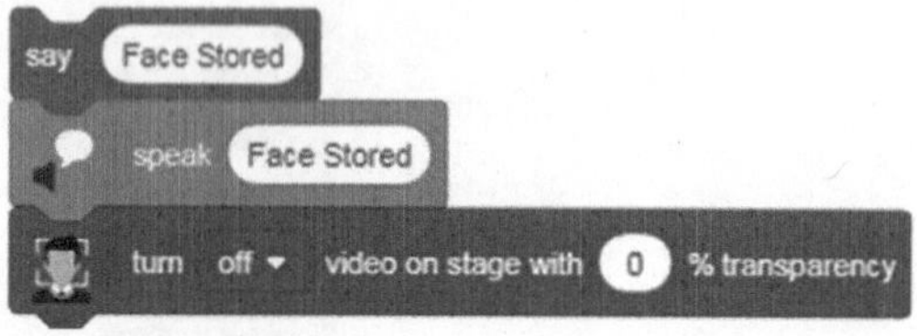

Step 5: Making Tobi Conversate

a To execute the program click the green flag, place a when flag clicked hat block from the Events palette.

b Do not open the camera, place the turn on video on stage with 0 % transparency block and choose off from the drop-down.

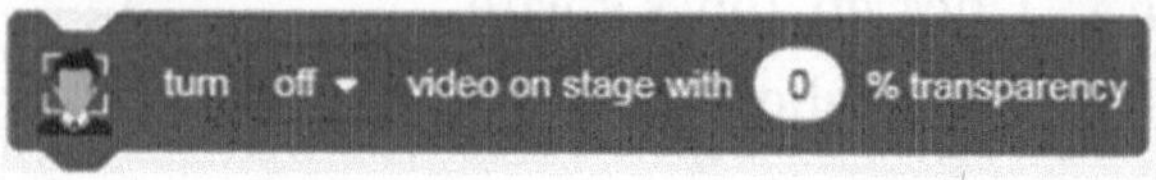

c From the text-to-speech palette, place a set voice to block and choose tenor from the drop-down.

d Now, to make sure that the door is closed, we need to make it as the default backdrop. Thus, from the looks palette, place a switch backdrop to block and choose door_1 from the drop-down.

e Now, let's make Tobi conversate.

f Place a say block from the Looks palette, and write Hello! I am Tobi in the space given.

g To make Tobi say it out loud, place speak block from the text-to-speech palette.

h To make the door as if it is closed every time the user clicks on green flag, go the backdrop, drag and drop when flag clicked hat block.

i Place switch backdrop block from the Looks palette and choose door_1 from the drop-down.

j The entire face recongition and the door sequence happen, when we press the blue button.

k Duplicate the above two blocks and write Please press the blue button to access the door in both the space given.

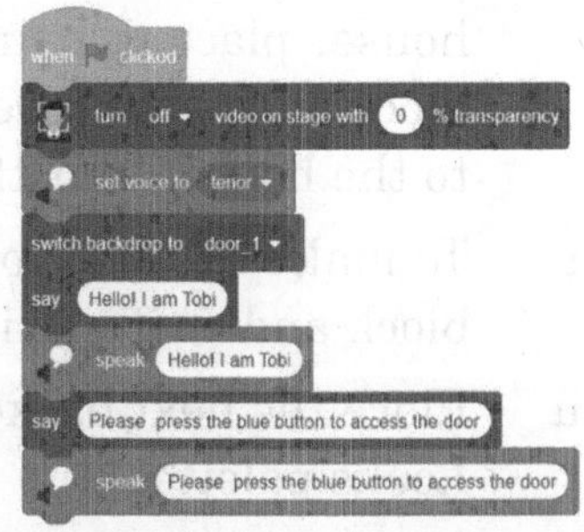

Step 6: Unlocking the Door Using Face Detection

a When the sprite is clicked, message will be broadcasted that the user is trying to access the door.

b Place when this sprite clicked hat block from the Events palette.

c And the broadcast block.

d Write Door Access as the new message in the drop-down of the broadcast block.

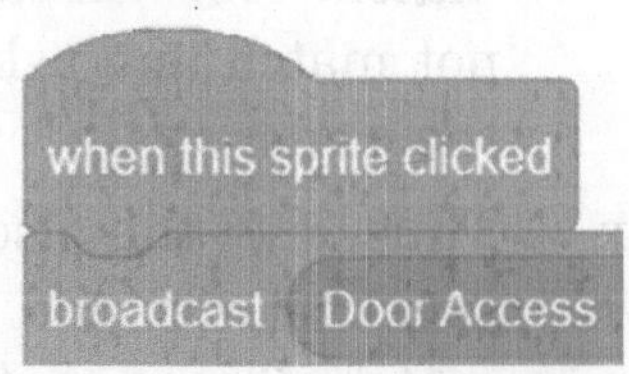

e Now, that the button is pressed, let's make the script for what happens to the door.

f Go back to the Tobi Sprite.

g Drag and drop the broadcast message hat block and choose Door Access from the drop-down.

h Make Tobi to guide the user and ask user to look into the camera.

i To do this place the say and the speak block and write "Please look into the camera" in both the spaces given.

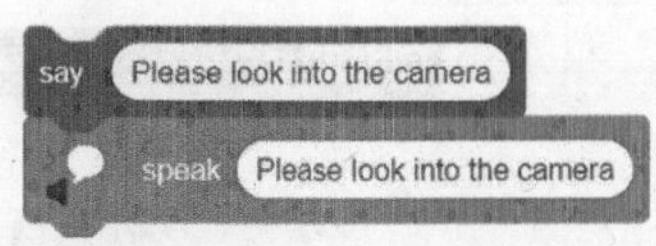

j Turn On the camera.

k Place the turn on video on stage with 0 % transparency block.

l To make camera to analyze, add a wait block from the Controls palette and write 3 in the space given.

m Let's ask the user to wait for a little while.

n Duplicate the pair of say and speak block and write Analysing in both.

o Now, to match up the face with the one stored in the class, place the do face matching on camera block from the Artificial Intelligence palette.

p In case, if the face is matched, Tobi will say that the face matched and the door to open.

q Place an if-else block from the Events palette.

r Place is 1 class detected from the Artificial Intelligence palette.

s To make the Tobi say that the face Matched and we are welcome to the house, place a pair of say and speak block and write Face matched! Welcome to the house! In both the spaces given.

t To make the Door open. Place a repeat block and write 12 in the space given.

u Place the next backdrop block from the Looks palette.

v To make the backdrop change visible place a wait of 0.1 seconds.

w Now, In case if the faces does not match. Tobi will say that the Face does not match and ask the user to contact the owner again.

x Thus, into the else arm place say and speak block and write "Face didn't match, Please contact the owner or try again." in both the spaces.

Script

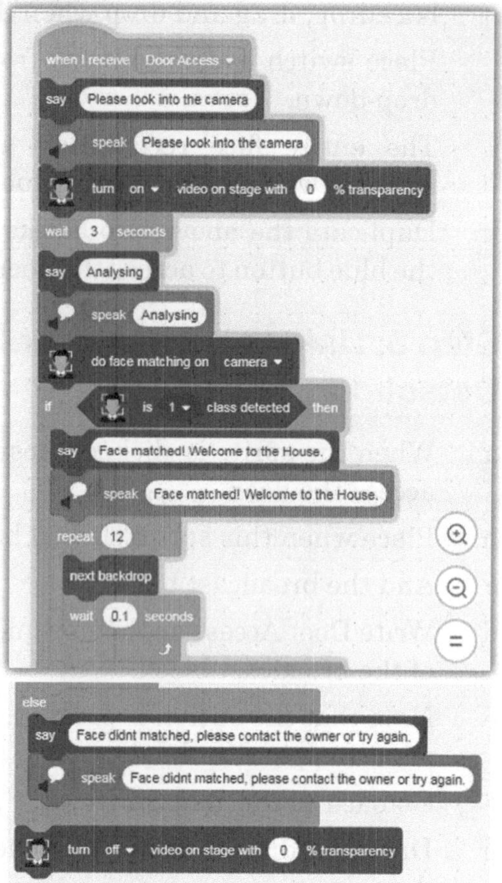

Output

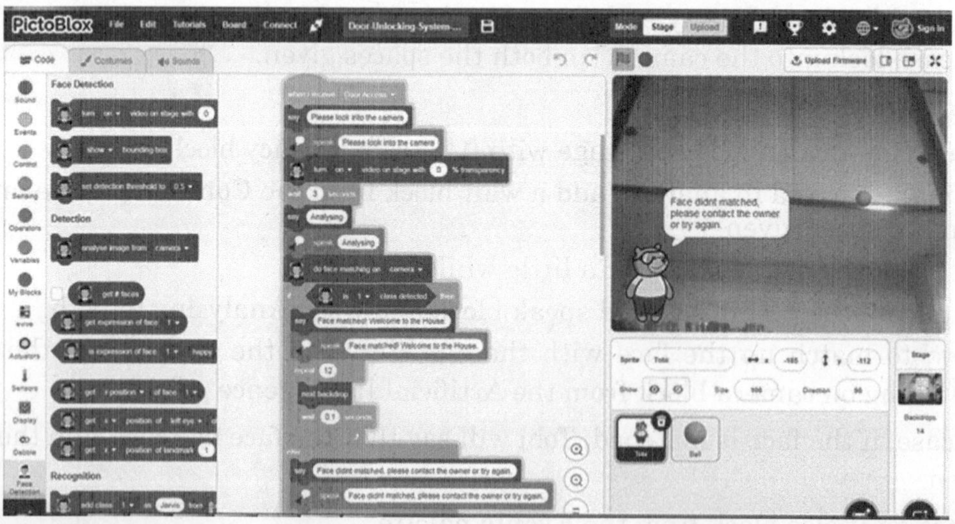

Sample Paper

Sample Paper

Time: 2 hours **Marks: 50**

A. Multiple choice questions. **1x10=10**

1. Artificial intelligence (AI) is an intelligence which is demonstrated by:
   a. Machines b. Humans
   c. Pets d. Homes
2. Modern machine capabilities explain that AI include in:
   a. Understanding human speech
   b. Competing at the highest level in strategic game systems (chess)
   c. Automatically operating cars
   d. All of the above
3. Artificial Intelligence is when a computer program or machine can:
   a. Think b. Learn
   c. Both a and b d. None of the above
4. With AI we have an algorithm or a _______ for the purpose of marketing a brand or a company.
   a. Machine b. Computer
   c. Bot d. Pet
5. Smart homes are homes that have all the ______ and security systems which are controlled by the owner with the click of button.
   a. electronic devices b. mechanical devices
   c. water devices d. none of the above
6. Home automation or domestics is a building automation for a home, known as:
   a. Smart home b. Smart house
   c. Both a and b d. None of the above
7. A home automation system will monitor and/or control the home attributes such as:
   a. Lighting b. Climate
   c. Entertainment systems d. All of the above
8. Various social themes, which every citizen must known to be a responsible citizen is:
   a. There must be No Poverty, No Hunger, No Poor health, No Poor education

b. There must be Gender equality, Clean water, Proper sanitation
c. Everyone must take proper action to protect climate
d. All of the above

9. With Sustainable Development Goals, you will:
   a Grow up in an interconnected and multicultural society in which you will learn about the various cultural norms.
   b Be an active participant in your communities and help the society to solve the world's biggest challenges.
   c Learn the various challenges such as sanitation, poverty, education, hunger.
   d All of the above

10. The Sustainable Development Goals (SDGs) are the collection of ________global goals which are designed to be a blueprint in order to achieve a better and the more sustainable future for all.
    a. 15 b. 16
    c. 17 d. 28

B. Fill in the blanks. **1×10=10**

Hints: Profit, sustainably, AI, solar system, Smart TV, Smart lighting, Smart thermostats, global challenges, big data, SDGs

1. Financial organizations are turning to AI to improve their stock trading performance and boost __________ .
2. AI can help farmers to get more from the land while using resources more __________ .
3. When it comes to saving our lives, a lot of organizations and medical care centres are relying on __________ .
4. Astronomers used Artificial Intelligence to sift through years of data obtained by the Kepler telescope in order to identify a distant eight-planet __________ .
5. __________ are connected to the internet to access on demand video and music.
6. __________ systems can detect when persons are in the room and adjust lighting as needed.
7. __________ connected with Wi-Fi, allowing users to schedule monitor and remotely control the home temperatures.

8. Artificial Intelligence helps us to solve complex and interrelated ________ which include hunger, change in climate and life on land.
9. AI processes are used to computerize the routine tasks, analyse the ________, generating the solutions to many sustainable development issues.
10. If an AI solution is designed in a well manner than it can play a transformative role in achieving, the________.

C. State whether the following statements are True or False. **1/2×10=5**

1. Natural language processing (NLP) describes the interaction among the human language and computers.
2. Computer vision is an interdisciplinary field that deals with how computers can be made to gain high-level understanding from digital images or videos.
3. Artificial Intelligence (AI) was first coined in 1999 at Dartmouth Conference.
4. Gamification is the process of adding game-like components to a task to encourage the participation of user participation.
5. Smart locks and garage-door openers can grant or deny access to visitors.
6. Pet care cannot be automated with connected feeders.
7. Smart security cameras through which you can monitor your homes when you away or on vacation.
8. Sustainable Development Goals as per the United Nations has eleven Sustainable Development Goals (SDGs), which come on effect from January 1, 2016.
9. The Sustainable Development Goals (SDGs) are the collection of 17 global goals which are designed to be a blueprint in order to achieve a better and the more sustainable future for all.
10. The SDGs, are set in 2015 by the United Nations General Assembly and is intended to be achieved by the year 2030, and is a part of UN Resolution 70/1, the 2030 Agenda.

D. Match the following. **1/2×10=5**

Column A	Column B
1. Artificial intelligence (AI)	i. watered by way of connected timers
2. Autonomous Vehicles	ii. Reduce the income inequality within and among the countries
3. Chatbots	iii. Natural language processing
4. NLP	iv. Build, promote resilient infrastructure, sustainable industrialization, and foster the innovation Siri, Cortana
6. Smart coffee makers	vi. Promote sustained, inclusive and sustainable economic growth for all
7. Smart refrigerators	vii. Cars that collects data from the vehicles radar,to produce control signals that operate the vehicle.
8. Decent Work and Economic Growth	viii. keep track of expiration dates
9. Industry, Innovation, and Infrastructure	ix. Intelligence demonstrated by machines
10. Reducing Inequality	xx. brew a fresh cup automatically at a programmed time

E. Answer the following questions. **(2×10=20)**

1. Why AI field was founded?
2. What is Artificial Intelligence?
3. What is the use of Social media in Artificial Intelligence?
4. How is Artificial Intelligence used in Games?
5. What is the need of Smart Home?
6. Write the use of smart coffee maker.
7. What is the use of inkle writer.
8. Explain Goal 5 of SDGs.
9. Explain the role of Artificial Intelligence in Sustainable Development.
10. Define Sustainable Development Goals (SDGs).

Notes

GLOSSARY

Artificial intelligence: Way in which a machine can copy the actions performed by humans and execute the task of humans.

Autonomous Vehicles/ Self driving cars/ Driverless cars : Self-driving cars have been a buzzword in the AI industry. The AI system collects data from the vehicles radar, cameras, GPS, and cloud services to produce control signals that operate the vehicle.

Chatbot: Software application that use Artificial intelligence and natural language processing to understand what a human wants, and guides them to their desired outcome.

Computer vision:
Interdisciplinary field that deals with how computers can be made to gain high-level understanding from digital images or videos.

Gamification: Process of adding game-like components to a task to encourage the participation of user participation.

Natural language processing (NLP): Describes the interaction among the human language and computers.

Smart home: Homes that have all the electronic devices and security systems which are controlled by the owner with the click of button.

Inklewriter: Freely available tool designed to allow anyone to write and publish interactive stories.

Notes

Chapterwise Solutions

Chapter 1

Brain Bot

A. 1. a 2. d 3. b 4. a 5. b

B. 1. Kepler 2. Self-driving 3. virtual 4. face verification 5. facial

C. 1. iii 2. ii 3. v 4. i 5. iv

Worksheet

A. 1. True 2. False 3. True 4. True 5. True

B. 1. virtual assistant 2. home attributes 3. speech 4. Cortana 5. Gamification

Quiz Card

1. d 2. b 3. b 4. d 5. d 6. c 7. d 8. d 9. a 10. a

Chapter 2

Brain Bot

A. 1. a 2. b 3. c 4. c 5. c

B. 1. button 2. control 3. smart home 4. home attributes 5. lighting

C. 1. iv 2. v 3. i 4. ii 5. iii

Worksheet

A. 1. True 2. False 3. True 4. True 5. False

B. 1. thermostats 2. locks 3. security cameras 4. Pet care 5. Houseplants

Quiz Card

1. b	2. b	3. d	4. a	5. a
6. a	7. a	8. a	9. d	10. b

Chapter 3

Brain Bot

A. 1. a 2. c 3. c 4. a 5. b

B. 1. January 1 2. poverty 3. hunger
4. increase 5. education

C. 1. iv 2. v 3. i 4. ii 5. iii

Worksheet

A. 1. True 2. True 3. False 4. False 5. True

B. 1. multicultural 2. 17 3. 2015
4. 70/1 5. Healthy lives

Quiz Card

1. d	2. d	3. d	4. d	5. b
6. d	7. c	8. b	9. c	10. a

Sample Paper

A. 1. a 2. d 3. c 4. c 5. a
6. c 7. c 8. d 9. d 10. d

B. 1. Profit 2. sustainably 3. AI
4. solar system 5. Smart TV 6. Smart lighting
7. Smart thermostats 8. global challenges 9. big data
10. SDGs

C. 1. True 2. True 3. False 4. True 5. True
6. False 7. True 8. False 9. True 10. True

D.

1. i	2. g	3. e	4. c	5. a
6. j	7. h	8. f	9. d	10. b

E. 1. AI field was founded on the assumption that human intelligence "can be so precisely described that a machine can be made to simulate it". Artificial Intelligence (AI) was first coined in 1956 at Dartmouth Conference by a cognitive scientist, John McCarthy, at the Dartmouth Conference.

2. Artificial intelligence (AI) refers to the simulation of human intelligence in the machines which are programmed to think like humans and mimic the actions of humans.
3. In social media platforms like Facebook, AI is used for face verification wherein machine learning and deep learning concepts are used to detect facial features and tag your friends.
4. Artificial Intelligence (AI) is used to generate responsive, adaptive or intelligent behaviours primarily in Non-Player Characters (NPCs) similar to human-like intelligence. Gaming actually creates the atmosphere that inspires learners to develop skills and build an emotional connect with the subject.
5. Smart homes are homes that have all the electronic devices and security systems which are controlled by the owner with the click of button.

   In Smart home:
   - From ventilation to heating, from security to air conditioning, everything will be in your control, at a distance of a button.
   - You click a button and you can have the entire control of which device would be working and which would stop working, right away.
6. Smart coffee makers can brew a fresh cup automatically at a programmed time.
7. inklewriter will help writers to tell interactive tales with the minimum of fuss. It will help you to write story in an organised manner, and to concentrate only on the writing.
8. Goal 5 of SDGs is Gender Equality, It's a stand-alone goal, which aims for women to receive the same attention as of men.
9. Artificial Intelligence helps us to solve complex and interrelated global challenges which include hunger, change in climate and life on land. AI processes are used to computerize the routine tasks, analyse the big data, generating the solutions to many sustainable development issues. If an AI solution is designed in a well manner than it can play a transformative role in achieving, the SDGs.
10. Sustainable Development Goals (SDGs) is the collection of 17 global goals which are designed to be a blueprint in order to achieve a better and the more sustainable future for all.

Notes